SETTING LIMITS

SETTING LIMITS

CONSTITUTIONAL
CONTROL
OF
GOVERNMENT

BY

LEWIS K. UHLER

REGNERY GATEWAY
WASHINGTON, D.C.

Library of Congress Cataloging-in-Publication Data

Uhler, Lewis K.
    Setting limits: constitutional control of government/by Lewis
K. Uhler.
        p.   cm.
    Includes index.
    ISBN 0-89526-756-X (pbk.)—ISBN 0-89526-546-X (cloth)
    1. Tax and expenditure limitations—United States.   2. Government
spending policy—United States.   3. Budget—Law and legislation—
United States.   I. Title.
HJ2381.U36   1989
336.3'9'0973—dc20   89-32293
                                                                CIP

Published in the United States by
Regnery Gateway
1130 17th Street, NW
Washington, D.C. 20036

Distributed to the trade by
National Book Network
4720-A Boston Way
Lanham, MD 20706

Manufactured in the United States of America

10 9 8 7 6 5 4 3 2 1

To my late father

JAMES CARVEL UHLER

who urged a mid-course correction
long before it became clear to others
that our Republic had lost its compass.

ACKNOWLEDGMENTS

THERE are many who have contributed to shaping this message. Their insights have proven invaluable to me, and I want to acknowledge their contributions: Martin Anderson; John C. Armor; Monroe Brown; James G. Campaigne; Robert B. Carleson; Cliff Christian; Alfred W. Cors, Jr.; Congressman Larry Craig; Robert Derr; M. Stanton Evans; Peter Fleming; Milton Friedman; Alfred J. Gagnon; Senator Phil Gramm; Robert B. Hawkins, Jr.; A. Lawrence Chickering, III; John T. Hay; Frank Hopkins; David A. Keene; Donald Lambro; William A. Niskanen; Daniel T. Oliver; Dick Phillips; Burt Pines; Alvin Rabushka; H. L. "Bill" Richardson; Hal G. Stratton; Wm. Craig Stubblebine; Ross Tharp.

To publisher Al Regnery, editor Harry Crocker, my assistant Diane Sekafetz, and thoughtful friend Sarah Hermann, I give special thanks.

My wife Cindy, sons Jim, Jon, Kirk, and Mark, and my mother Mavis have been constant sources of support and encouragement.

Lewis K. Uhler

CONTENTS

ABOUT THIS BOOK

THIS book has several stylistic features: We have sprinkled questions and answers—in the form of "Myths and Realities"—throughout the book to place in brief perspective many of the issues raised. We hope they are useful in gaining insight into the real Washington. At the end of several chapters we have included in slightly smaller type "postscripts" that contain material often reserved for an appendix. Yet the information is important to a complete appreciation of the issues developed in those chapters. To assist the reader and to avoid the inconvenience of moving from text to appendix and back again, we have chosen the postscript medium.

FOREWORD

WE who are fortunate enough to be citizens of the United States of America have long prided ourselves on having—in Abraham Lincoln's memorable words—a "government of the people, by the people, for the people." But do we?

"Of the people"—yes, if that means "over" the people. We have a government that has the power to govern its citizens: to require them to serve in the military, to obey a collection of laws that boggles the imagination in its complexity and extent, and to pay open and hidden taxes that enable governments at all levels to spend an amount equal to more than 40 percent of a year's national income.

"By the people"—hardly, if that means that the will of the public at large controls the actions of the government. Eighty-five percent of "the people" want the federal government to balance the budget, yet large deficits continue year after year. Nearly the same percentage of "the people" want the budget balanced by a reduction in spending rather than an increase of taxes. Yet their elected representatives year after year have increased spending and have tried hard, and mostly with success, to increase taxes while professing to reduce them. What percentage of "the people" do you suppose would answer "yes" to the question, "Are you getting your money's worth for the more than 40 percent of your income that governments at all levels are spending, supposedly on your behalf?"

"For the people"—clearly no, unless "the" is replaced by "some." Is it government "for the people" to require them to pay twice the world price for sugar in order to "protect" a handful of domestic producers of beet and cane sugar? To spend the taxpayers' money on both discouraging smoking and subsidizing the growing of tobacco? On both reducing the production of milk to make its price high and paying for school lunches to assure that children whose parents cannot afford to buy the high-priced milk get milk to drink?

Perfection is, of course, impossible, but these and numerous similar examples make it clear that we are very far indeed from Lincoln's ideal and, even more serious, have been moving farther from it in recent decades.

Nothing is more responsible for our growing departure from Lincoln's ideal than the nearly unlimited power of the Congress to spend and its ability to finance that spending without having to vote openly for additional taxes. Instead, it can finance that spending by hidden taxes, "taxation without representation"—printing money, letting inflation generate revenue through "bracket creep" and the repudiation of debt, and the even more insidious tax implicit in what are called "deficits."

The most promising alternative open to us as citizens to end the erosion of Lincoln's ideal is to adopt a constitutional amendment to require a balanced budget and to limit taxation. That is not a visionary dream. On the contrary, it came within an ace of being achieved in 1982, when the constitutionally-required two-thirds of the Senate and a majority, though not the necessary two-thirds, of the House voted for such an amendment. Had those few needed votes been garnered in the House, I am confident that the constitutionally-required three-quarters of the states would promptly have approved the amendment. In that case, we would now be operating under an excellent tax limitation/balanced budget amendment, and our fiscal affairs would already be in far healthier shape than they are now. Public support for the amendment is as strong as it has ever been. Only a final push is needed to make the dream a reality.

When such an amendment is adopted, there will be no doubt who deserves to be labelled its father. His name is Lewis Uhler. Since 1972, when he served as Chairman of then-California Governor Ronald Reagan's Tax Reduction Task Force, Lew Uhler has tirelessly pursued the goal of ending runaway government taxing and spending. He early decided that a national citizens' effort was required, not a government project, and that the effort should not be restricted to one state. He thereupon organized the National Tax Limitation Committee, supporting it, in its early years, out of his own pocket and by his volunteer efforts. He has remained the moving spirit and driving force in an enterprise that has grown to a major national crusade supported actively by millions of his fellow citizens and many of their organizations. It has been a privilege to observe his tireless dedication to a cause that he believes in with all his heart.

This book is another contribution by Lew to the cause. In it he explains clearly and simply for his fellow citizens how we have gotten into the fix we are in; why the constitutional route is the only effective way out; and how we can successfully pursue that route.

This book is for every citizen who would answer "no" to the question, "Are you getting your money's worth for the more than 40 percent of your income that governments at all levels are spending supposedly on your behalf?" If enough of them read it, Lew's dream will quickly become a reality.

Milton Friedman
Senior Research Fellow
Hoover Institution

INTRODUCTION

IN this bicentennial period of homage to the Founders, it is not inappropriate to inquire what it was they thought they were founding. To the extent we have strayed from their conception, we must ask why—and how. If we don't like the results, we are obliged to put things right.

The Founders were trying to create a "level playing field" (to steal from the contemporary vernacular of Washington) in which government's role was as a neutral party or referee, not as a player. The "levelness," or equality, they were seeking was that of *opportunity*—not *outcome*. That is *the* crucial distinction that transcends every other consideration.

To confirm this distinction, let's look closely at the Constitution. The federal government was to protect us from enemies domestic and foreign (so there would be a field to play on), provide courts to adjudicate disputes (instead of trial by battle), provide a common currency (so we would not have to barter and we could rely on established monetary values), establish a postal network (to facilitate communication at a distance in the only means then available—via the written word), and prohibit tariffs and trade barriers between the states (so that commerce could develop freely based on competition, not parochial protectionism). These delegated powers, and a few others, were the extent of it. The balance of the Constitution not dealing with structure and administration consisted of proscriptions on the activities and powers of the federal government. The Bill of Rights constituted a further limitation on the power of the federal government *vis-à-vis* individual citizens. The focus was on individuals and individual rights, not on groups or classes. And the nature of that individual focus was protection *from* government intrusion.

Nowhere in the Bill of Rights is there any mention of government being responsible to do anything *for* an individual, such as having an affirmative duty to support him and to guarantee him a living. Certainly there was no hint that government would be authorized to coerce one individual to support another through government taxation and redistribution. The notion of government—especially the federal government—acting as *big brother* was alien to those who met at Philadelphia.

It is clear that the Founders sought to facilitate the exercise of freedom, not create a federal structure that would inhibit it. They did not intend that the power of the federal government be used as an instrument of coercion to the detriment of some and the benefit of others.

Unfortunately, the present-day federal government bears absolutely no resemblance to that fashioned by our Founders. It is an active player in redistributing the wealth of the nation. It has done exactly what Thomas Jefferson complained of in the Declaration of Independence when in his list of grievances he said of King George III, "He has erected a multitude of new offices, and sent hither swarms of officers to harass our people, and eat out their substance."

The honest, hardworking citizen, who is only marginally concerned with politics or political ideology, is necessarily preoccupied with work, family, friends, religious and social obligations, golf, Little League, service clubs, holidays, weddings—all the time-consuming challenges of life. He gets his news and information in bits and pieces—television, newspaper headlines, gossip, drive-time radio information "bites." He tries to fit it into the framework of the way our representative government is supposed to work à la eleventh grade civics. But it doesn't fit. His government is doing all kinds of things that seem to make no sense, many of which run counter to his own beliefs. "Somehow, my government has left me," he says.

If you suggest that he get active in politics to correct the situation, you will very likely be told that he doesn't want to get involved. He doesn't realize that he is already involved, whether he likes it or not. He might as well face that fact squarely.

We know there's a problem, but we must understand its nature. From that understanding comes a solution. And that solution befits our bicentennial, because it is constitutional in nature.

Setting limits on Washington—more precisely, restoring limits—is our bicentennial challenge. Not many decades ago, Washington was known as a "sleepy southern town." Now it is a "boom town"—at the expense of the rest of the nation. Our objective should be to thrust Washington, D.C., into a permanent recession—that would be our best assurance of a prosperous America.

Lewis K. Uhler
February 1989

PART I

THE NUMBERS IN PERSPECTIVE

CHAPTER 1

NATIONAL TAXES

> ... the Pharisees and the teachers of the law who belonged to their sect complained to his disciples, "Why do you eat and drink with *tax collectors* and sinners?" Jesus answered them, "It is not the healthy who need a doctor, but the sick. I have not come to call the righteous, but sinners, to repentance.
>
> (Luke 5:30–32)

AMERICA was born of a tax rebellion, with the cry, "Taxation without representation is tyranny." Comparing England's oppression of the colonies with our current tax load, I sometimes wonder what the fuss was about.

Adam Smith, the great eighteenth century economist, reviewed colonial government expenditures and reached this conclusion: "All the different civil establishments in North America . . . did not, before the commencement of the present disturbances, cost the inhabitants over 64,700 pounds a year."[1] The "present disturbances" Smith refers to was the American War of Independence, protesting the intolerable tax burden of—well, how much was it?

The total cost of administering the colonies then was about $2 million a year, or 67 cents per person per year. When our nation was founded, the federal government spent about $3 million a year—about $1 per person. By 1910, after 120 years of operation, our federal government spent just over $600 million—about $6.75 per person.[2] (There had been modest inflation in the intervening years.)

THE TAX EXPLOSION

Then came the federal income tax (Sixteenth Amendment) in 1913. The impact on the income tax began somewhat slowly. By 1929 the federal government was spending $3 billion *per year* (about $29 per person). Now the federal government spends $3 billion *every day* (over $4,000 per person per year). Even after we adjust for inflation, total federal taxes have increased about 6000 percent since adoption of the federal income tax.[3] The share of the Gross National Product (GNP) spent by the federal government has grown from three percent to about 24 percent—eight times since 1929.

Taxation *with representation* has turned into a nightmare. Government is the "senior partner" in every American business, and its tax burden is the largest item in every working American's budget. WE pay more for "being governed" than for food, clothing, and shelter combined. Total taxes in 1929—federal, state and local—equalled about 10 percent of our national income. Today combined taxes are well over 40 percent of the earnings of our nation.

WHAT IS A TRILLION?

It is nearly impossible to describe how much the federal government "liberates" from the working people of America each year. The numbers are staggering even to the

---

MYTH

High taxes are the price we must pay for our free society.

REALITY

High taxes *are* a threat to a free society and personal liberty. The condition that distinguishes a free man from a slave is dominion over himself and the fruits of his labor. Every dollar transferred through taxes takes power from the taxpaying citizen and gives it to the government.

---

politicians who have imposed the taxes. What is a trillion dollars—$1,000,000,000,000—other than "something big?" That's how much our federal government is now spending each year. Does it help knowing that it is a thousand billion or a million million? Probably not.

TAX INCREASE TREACHERY

Resistance to tax increases has risen steadily, aided by the policies and rhetoric of Ronald Reagan and abetted by the "read-my-lips" promise of President George Bush. Congress has had to move demagoguery from an art to a science to increase its revenues.

The experience of the so-called "windfall profits tax" imposed on oil companies a few years ago points up one of the favorite tricks of politicians seeking "easy marks" on whom to levy new taxes without inviting the wrath of the general public. If Congress can shift the focus from taxes to morality, presumably addressing some overriding issue of the moment, you'll get tax increase for sure.

In 1984, we experienced a tax increase that was advertised as a "down payment on the deficit." Remember? The politicians, however, used the new revenues not to reduce the deficit but to accommodate greater spending. Fiscal year 1985 saw one of the greatest increases of spending in our history—from $852 to $946 billion—more than an 11 percent increase.[4]

"NO NEW TAXES"

The last thing our nation needs is another tax increase. President Bush is absolutely right in his commitment: "No new taxes." There is only one problem—tax revenues are growing faster than our economy *without a tax increase*.

During the mid-1980s, taxes as a share of GNP remained in the 18 percent range, where they had been throughout the decade of the 1970s. But recently we have crept back into the 19 percent range. Tax revenues in the 1989 fiscal year are estimated to increase by $60 billion over 1988—more than seven percent—and by over $80 billion in 1990.[5]

Bottom Line: Tax revenues are growing—without a tax increase—and are growing faster than our economy.

Even after "indexing" the personal income tax rates for inflation and adopting a two-tier "flat tax" in the 1986 Tax Reform Act, tax revenues are growing faster than our ability to pay. We are transferring more and more of our income and wealth to Washington. There is a structural

MYTH

If we increase taxes, we can get rid of the deficit.

REALITY

We've had major tax increases over the past several years, and yet during this same period we have experienced the largest deficits in our history. The 1984 tax increase was widely publicized as a "downpayment on the deficit." Remember?

Immediately following that tax increase—during fiscal year 1985—we experienced the single largest *spending increase* in recent memory. Federal outlays went from $852 billion in 1984 to $946 billion in 1985, more than an 11 percent increase.

Did that tax increase bring down the deficit? No, the deficit zoomed from $185 billion to $212 billion that year.

It has become painfully clear that Congress does not use tax increases to reduce spending. Tax increases merely accommodate greater spending, which in turn leads to more tax increases.

Only control of spending will halt this vicious circle and enable us to reduce the deficits.

flaw in our existing tax system. Tax rate reduction should be the order of the day.

Brutus, the anti-federalist, writing during the debates on ratifying the Constitution, warned:

> The power to tax, exercised without limitation, will introduce itself into every corner of the city, and country—it will enter the house of every gentleman, watch over his cellar, wait upon his cook in the kitchen, follow the servants into the parlor, preside over the table, and note down all he eats and drinks; it will take cognizance of the professional man in his office, or study; it will watch the merchant in the counting house, or any store; it will follow the mechanic to his shop, and in his work, and will haunt him in his family, and in his bed; it will be a constant companion of the industrious farmer in all his labor . . . ; it will penetrate into the most obscure cottage; and finally it will light upon the head of every person in the United States. To all these different classes of people, and in all these circumstances, in which it will attend them, the language in which it will address them, will be GIVE, GIVE."[6]

MYTH

Deficits are the result of Reagan's tax cuts.

REALITY

It's not tax cuts but dramatic spending increases that caused our deficits. Tax reductions have merely offset social security tax increases.

Recently, total taxes have been inching up from 18 percent of GNP and are now about 19 percent. Spending, which zoomed to nearly 25 percent of GNP, has been growing somewhat more slowly than taxes. Tax receipts of the federal government have increased by more than $60 billion in 1989 and are projected to grow by more than $80 billion in 1990, even with indexation of the personal income tax and the Tax Reform Act of 1986.

CHAPTER 2

PERSONAL TAXES

Noah must have taken into the ark two taxes, one male and one female. And did they multiply bountifully.
(Will Rogers)

WE taxpayers, we who bear the entire federal tax burden, know the problem better than anyone else. We feel it firsthand. We see it in the "deductions" that government snips from every paycheck. We curse it every April 15.

The burden is staggering. Federal taxes in 1989 ($965 billion) represent a bill of more than $3,900 for every man, woman, and child in America. On top of that, more than $700 per person is borrowed and spent by the federal government. For a family of four, the total taxes and money borrowed by the federal government exceeds $18,000 per year.

You may not pay that much directly, but stop and think about it. In the price of every good and service you buy are the corporate taxes paid by the manufacturer, the excise taxes charged, and the price of the interest rate influenced by federal borrowing. Yes, we pay, whether we can always see it or not. If not us, who? The rich? If we were to tax away *all* the income of *all* the "very rich," it would pay for only a few days of federal spending.

WHO PAYS?

Although high earners do pay a higher proportion of income taxes, the majority of income-related taxes falls on those earning under $40,000 a year.[1] Middle- and lower-income workers bear, proportionately, a far greater share of those taxes designated for social security. Social security taxes are second only to personal income taxes as the federal government's largest single source of revenue.[2]

Piled atop the personal income and social security taxes are federal corporation taxes, capital gains taxes, gasoline taxes, "luxury" taxes, liquor taxes, tobacco taxes, and a host of excises, customs, tariffs, licenses, and fees.

Does someone else pay these taxes—perhaps the huge multinational corporations? CORPORATIONS, WHETHER LARGE OR SMALL, DON'T PAY TAXES—THEY JUST COLLECT TAXES. Those taxes translate into lower dividends to their stockholders, lower wages for their employees, and higher prices for their customers. The politicians try to fool us into thinking "greedy business people" will pay, but the taxes fall on all of us in the form of incomes that are lower than they would be without the taxes.

TAX GROWTH OFF THE CHART

The *growth* of the federal tax burden for each American over the last 200 years is arrayed on the accompanying chart. To be as accurate as possible, we have adjusted the numbers to account for inflation (using constant 1967 dollars) and for the changes in our population (we started

MYTH

Taxes should be shifted to the wealthy and the corporations. That will help low-and moderate-income families.

REALITY

We have already shifted much of the tax burden to the wealthy. The top one percent of taxpayers pay 22 percent of all personal income taxes; the bottom 50 percent of taxpayers pay only seven percent. It is middle-income Americans who continue to pay the bulk of federal taxes.

Shifting taxes to corporations is a fantasy. Businesses do not pay taxes; only people pay them. An increase in corporate income tax, for example, is paid by *customers* in the form of increased prices, *employees* in the form of lower wages, and *shareholders* in decreased dividends. So *we the people* pay for the tax increase, but the politicians like it because the taxes are rendered less visible to us.

Shifting taxes to business reduces investment and, hence, wealth creation and jobs. *Shifting* the tax burden is not the answer; *reducing* the tax burden is. We should not be seduced into playing the tax-shifting game. The big spenders want us to fight among ourselves. Ben Franklin was right: "If we don't hang together, we'll all hang separately."

with three million people and now have approximately
245 million). As you can see, the federal tax burden for
each of us has gone (literally) off the chart. If you were to
add state and local taxes, the results would be even worse.

As the chart demonstrates rather dramatically, the tax
burden of each American held relatively constant from our
founding until the Civil War, and at a slightly higher but
constant plateau until passage of the income tax (Sixteenth) amendment in 1913. Once the potential of the
income tax became reality in Washington, the tax burden
each of us has borne has increased virtually unabated. We
abandoned the protection against "direct" taxes the Founders wisely incorporated into the Constitution. To repair
the damage we must resort to constitutional reform.

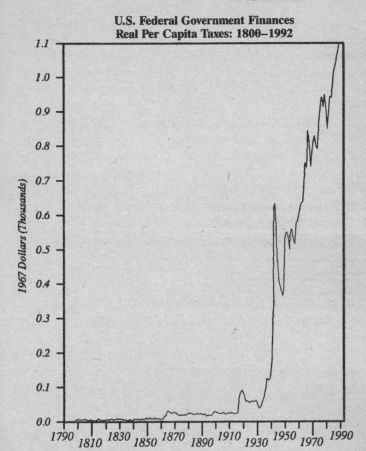

U.S. Federal Government Finances
Real Per Capita Taxes: 1800–1992

1967 Dollars (Thousands)

Year

Source: Wm. Craig Stubblebine Von Tobel
Professor of Economics
Claremont McKenna College
Claremont, California

CHAPTER 3

THE NATIONAL DEBT

> I can scarcely contemplate a greater calamity that
> could befall this country, than be loaded with a debt
> exceeding their ability ever to discharge. If this be a
> just remark, it is unwise and improvident to vest in the
> general government a power to borrow at discretion,
> without any limitation or restriction.
>
> (*Brutus,* Anti-Federalist, *1787–88*)[1]

OUR (cash) national debt now stands at over *$2.8 trillion*.
This represents a mortgage for every man, woman, and
child in America of more than $10,000, or more than
$20,000 for every working American; $40,000 for a family of four.

For fiscal year 1989, interest payments (gross) on the
accumulated debt of the United States government exceeded $220 billion.[2] Interest alone is the third largest
item in the federal budget, just behind defense and social
security. Your share of that annual interest cost is nearly
$900. That's what it takes to service the federal mortgage.
Bringing it even closer to home, *the interest share for a
family of four is well over $60 each and every week—just
to pay the interest on the (cash) national debt.*

Why do we refer to the "cash" national debt? Because
that's the debt we keep track of on the books of the United

States—the one for which the Treasury Department issues T-bills and other debt instruments—the one we have to pay interest on each and every year to keep the federal government out of bankruptcy. Our attention is always focused on that debt because the federal government keeps its books on a cash accounting basis, rather than on the accrual basis required of large companies and most everyone else. On an accrual accounting basis, the national debt is much larger. That method takes into account the promises that we have made for future expenditures—to military and civilian retirees of the federal government, to social security beneficiaries, and for other obligations the government has guaranteed to pay.

When you buy an insurance policy, or an annuity, or receive a private pension plan, there is a legal requirement that the company managers handling the funds invest and build the fund so it's there when you call upon it. If they don't do so, they can go to jail. If the same standards had been applied over the years to those in Congress who have voted for benefits but have failed to provide for raising the money necessary to fund them, we'd have generations of "public servants" behind bars.

SOCIAL SECURITY "BORROWING" DANGEROUS

Right now the social security system is running a surplus—more than $50 billion in 1989, $60 billion in 1990, $80 billion in 1991, and on and on. But that surplus is being used by the federal government to make up for excessive expenditures elsewhere. The treasury issues special federal government bonds to the social security system for that difference and *accrues but does not pay the interest on them*.

When the day of reckoning arrives and the working Americans who paid into social security prepare to retire, neither the principal nor interest will be there for them. They and those then in the work force will have to be taxed more to pay for social security benefits then due.

TRILLIONS OF DOLLARS OF FUTURE LIABILITIES

There are various estimates of the dollar value of the so-called "unfunded" liabilities of the federal government—promised future payments that have not been funded. No one has been able to calculate accurately the extent of such liabilities, but they number in the trillions of dollars. They include the contingent liabilities arising from savings & loan and bank deposit insurance, student loans, farm credit, and a stunning array of off-budget financing. The savings & loan debacle is an all-too-chilling example of these financial time bombs. Retirement obligations to federal civilian and military personnel, for which no investment has been provided, simply compound the problem.

As the number of workers declines relative to the number of people who have claims on the federal treasury, there is going to be a terrible crunch. And the politicians who launched these politically attractive but devastatingly costly obligations will all be dead and gone.

There are those who claim that we need not worry about the national debt. "We just owe it to ourselves," they say. They neglect to mention that we still must pay the carrying costs—interest. Others suggest that the annual deficit is declining as a share of our GNP so we can ignore it. Let's take a look at a simple chart and see what the facts really are:

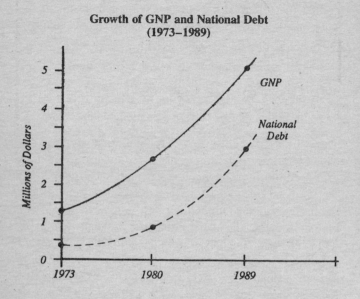

Growth of GNP and National Debt
(1973–1989)

Between 1973 and 1989, the GNP grew about four times—from $1.28 trillion to $5.12 trillion. During the same period the national debt grew about six times—from less than half a trillion dollars to $2.86 trillion. As a percentage of GNP, the national debt has grown from 36 percent to 56 percent.[3] *We've been increasing our debt load faster than we've been increasing our income.* That's why our interest payments have climbed from about seven percent of our national budget to 15 percent.

All the fancy talk about deficits not mattering can't alter history nor the specter of an ever-growing debt burden.

MYTH

Don't worry about the national debt. We just owe it to ourselves.

REALITY

This was one of the favorite shibboleths of our Keynesian economists. It implies that the debt is a fiction, as if we could just as well ignore it as honor it. This flip, arrogant approach to the fiscal policy of our nation has pushed us to the brink. Interest (gross) on the national debt alone exceeds $220 billion for fiscal year 1989, the third-largest item in our budget. We have reached the undreamed-of situation in which our national debt has grown at a greater rate than the real growth of our economy.

Just because the deficit shrinks one year as a percentage of GNP does not put things right. The fact that the deficit-to-GNP ratio for 1989 is about three percent, down from a historic peacetime high of six percent in the mid-1980s, is hardly a source of jubilation. That ratio was only 1.2 percent as recently as 1973.[4] The deficit remains substantially higher than contemplated by Gramm-Rudman-Hollings (GRH) when that law was passed in 1985.

Deficits *do* matter. Ask the young people who have to foot the bill.

PART II

HOW WE GOT IN THIS FIX

CHAPTER 4

Opening the Door

> I . . . place economy among the first and most important of republican virtues, and public debt as the greatest of dangers to be feared. . . . And to preserve (our) independence, we must not let our rulers load us with perpetual debt. We must make our election between economy and liberty, or profusion and servitude.
>
> *(Thomas Jefferson)*[1]

TOO much government is the problem, and we wouldn't have it if we had listened to Thomas Jefferson. We have been entreated to trade some of our freedom for security and have found that government has made us both less free and less secure.

Our government, as befits a free people, used to be the smallest and least meddlesome in any modern country. But now it has become everything that Jefferson feared: a spendthrift leviathan that squanders our labor and loads us with a mountainous public debt. Over the last half-century, no matter the party in power, our government has confiscated a greater share of our national productivity, leaving a smaller piece of the pie for the rest of us. As public spending increases, personal freedom shrinks. We Americans, thinking ourselves still free, actually must work longer each year to pay for *our* government than the medieval serfs had to work for *their* feudal lords!

Just how we've come to be in this fiscal fix is a head-scratcher for most Americans. And certainly it should be. When at least three-quarters of the people find deficits totally distasteful and demand a balanced budget amendment to end them,[2] how can they continue? How can it be that during the administration of a fiscally conservative president who really wanted to end deficits, the red ink got larger, not smaller. To find the answer, we must review a little history.

ADOPTION OF THE INCOME TAX—1913

The first step was giving the federal government virtually unlimited access to the "fuel" of government—money. Until the Sixteenth Amendment was passed in 1913, there was *no income tax* (except for a brief period during the Civil War). Duties and excise taxes constituted the major revenue sources for the federal government. The Founding Fathers did not want the federal government to be able to tax the people of this country *directly*. They did not want to give it the power which direct taxation would accommodate. The Sixteenth Amendment provided the *source* of the funds for big government and made big spending a possibility.

BREACH OF THE UNWRITTEN RULE AGAINST DEFICITS

During the first 150 years or so in the life of the American Republic, there was an unwritten but solemnly honored rule that while the nation might run deficits during wartime, the debt should be retired during the ensuing peace.

That pledge prevailed through the 1920s as the debt of World War I was being retired. Only as we endured the Great Depression was this unwritten constitutional rule against deficits ruptured.

EXPLOSION OF WASHINGTON ACTIVITIES

In the late 1930s, another critically important element came into play: the scope of federal activities became virtually limitless. A series of U.S. Supreme Court decisions eroded the time-honored constitutional barriers against federal encroachment into areas of human activity historically reserved to states, local government, private individuals, and private organizations. Congress happily took advantage by creating a blizzard of alphabet-soup programs and agencies.

WITHHOLDING TAX IMPOSED

As the personal income tax began to reach into the pocketbooks of middle America, there was a practical limit to the amount that could be extracted from most working people at a once-a-year tax time. In 1944, the big spenders invented tax withholding, making the employer the tax collector. This reduced the pain of the income tax on the theory that "what you don't receive you won't miss."

The withholding schedules have been designed to "overwithhold," qualifying most taxpayers for a refund. The psychology of April 15th has been converted from universal agony to a second "Christmas" for a sizable percentage of taxpayers who eagerly await their tax refunds. For 1988, the IRS expected to refund an average of more than $900 on 75 percent of the anticipated 109 million returns. That amounts to about $75 billion of overwithholding, nearly 20 percent of all personal income taxes for the year.[3]

PROGRESSIVE TAX STRUCTURE— "BRACKET CREEP"

The *progressive* nature of the income tax rate structure was the final element in making big government possible. As average incomes increased, taxpayers were pushed into ever higher tax brackets. This in turn gave Congress a greater share of the national income without ever having to vote to raise taxes. Commonly referred to as "bracket creep," this phenomenon became explosive when the fires of inflation were ignited.

The money poured into the U.S. Treasury—and, of course, Washington found exciting new ways to spend it. Fiscal discipline became the casualty.

CHAPTER 5

ONCE THE DOOR WAS OPENED

No man's life, liberty or property is safe while the
legislature is in session.

(Judge Gideon J. Tucker, NY, ca. 1866)

IN Washington, D.C., at the corner of 17th Street and
Pennsylvania Avenue, just opposite the West Wing of the
White House, is an ornate structure known as the Old
Executive Office Building. It recently celebrated its 100th
anniversary. When the building was completed in 1886, it
housed the Departments of Navy and War (the entire
military command structure of the United States), as well
as all of the Department of State. Although the population
of the United States has increased only fourfold in the
intervening years, the Old Executive Office Building is
now not even large enough to hold the people who serve
on the President's staff.

In the 75 years since the income tax was authorized, the
U.S. population has increased about two-and-one-half
times, but the number of federal civilian employees has
increased nearly 10 times, and federal taxes have increased over a thousand times.[1]

It is human nature to accept that which exists as if it had
always been. Nothing could be more inapplicable to
Washington. In a relatively short period—less than 75

years—Washington has undergone a transformation of incredible proportions. It has gone from a tranquil southern town that "consumed" about three percent of the national income, to the "center of empire," à la Rome, that controls about one-quarter of what we Americans produce each year. Let's check the facts.

TURN OF THE CENTURY—
A LEAN WASHINGTON

In the early years of this century, Congress appropriated about a half-billion dollars a year to operate the entire federal government, usually with a surplus, because the federal budget was reasonably lean.[2]

Senators and Representatives had no offices (the first Senate and House office buildings were completed in 1908); they did their work in the House or Senate chambers, in committee hearings, or in the lobbies within the Capitol building itself.[3] They were paid $5,000 a year and regularly engaged in gainful employment back home.[4] And their staffs were small. There were only 70 personal staff members for 96 Senators. This means that *some Senators had no staff at all*. In 1914, the personal staff, plus the staff of the standing committees in both the House and Senate, totaled fewer than 400 people to serve the 531 members of the House and Senate.[5]

COST OF CONGRESS SOARS

Then came Big Government, which took root during the Wilsonian era, matured during the New Deal, and went on a rampage with Lyndon Johnson's "War on Poverty." The budget for the Congress itself has tracked this explosive growth in spending. In 1914, the cost of operating the Congress was $7.5 *million, 7.5 cents* per U.S. citizen. That cost has risen to $2.2 billion in 1989—a whopping nine *dollars* for every one of us in our nation—just to operate a Congress that has only four more members than it did in 1914.[6] Or to look at it another way, each Senator and Representative cost taxpayers $14 *thousand* for the entire year of 1914; in 1989 that annual cost had risen to well over $4 *million*—a 30,000 percent increase—to support each Senator and Representative.

CONGRESSIONAL PERKS

The part-time "public service" contemplated by our Founding Fathers has been supplanted by full-time, career-oriented Representatives and Senators who, by and large, reside in Washington. They enjoy ever-increasing salaries, the 1989 pay raise defeat being a rare exception. They are entitled to unlimited "franked" (postage-free) mail designed to keep Senators' and Representatives' names before their constituents. In election year 1988, members of Congress distributed 600 million pieces of mail, most of them unsolicited "newsletters"—12,000 pieces for every letter Congress receives. This cost taxpayers well over $100 million.[7]

Other "perks" available to members of Congress include various free medical services, free gym facilities, free parking in Capitol garages and at Washington airports, numerous free trips—and the list goes on and on. The pension system is among the most generous in the nation, allowing many congressmen to receive not only much more than they've paid in, but more per year than their current annual salary.

STAFF FIT FOR A KING

From the turn of the century when Senators and Representatives had no private offices and few staffers, Congress now occupies six huge office buildings and surrounds each Senator with an average of 40 personal staff, each Representative with just under 20. Add other support staff from committees, the General Accounting Office, researchers in the Library of Congress, officers of the House and Senate and you have a grand total of approximately 38,000 congressional employees—over 70 staff and support personnel for every member of Congress.[8]

An increase in the number of staff has meant an increase in the quantity of legislation, fulfilling the promise that "work will fill the time available." Substantial reliance on staff is the rule, not the exception. Because of the virtually unlimited scope of Congress's activities, and the workload it has generated, staff members heavily influence policy decisions.

Mark Brisnow, a 13-year veteran staffer to three senators, three congressmen, and three different committees, confessed about the 1987 congressional session:

The 535 members of the U.S. Congress accomplished very little this year, and it took 20,000 staffers to help them do it. Over the last 15 years the size of the congressional staff has increased threefold. . . . When I arrived on Capitol Hill as a junior aide for Senator Hubert Humphrey in 1975, the Watergate scandal had convinced congressmen that they needed to "assert" themselves against the Imperial Presidency. How? By hiring more staff, naturally. . . . I came to learn there are all sorts of ways congressional staffers serve themselves or their bosses but not always the national interest. Like hyperactive stockbrokers who buy and sell for quick commissions regardless of the long-term profit to their clients, congressional staffers become adept at the art of "churning." The result is ever more friction among members, factions, parties, and branches of government. Congress has no less than 150 subcommittees, and each one has its own staff that must justify its existence. . . . Many staffers draft bills just to raise a congressman's profile—and attract contributions from special-interest groups. Many of these bills have absolutely no chance of passing and in fact, of the 6,504 bills introduced this year, a mere 197 passed. . . . But aren't staffers essential to helping congressmen comprehend the increasingly complex and broad-ranging issues that they face? One might guess so, but actually lawmakers use staffers as a crutch. Why should a congressman master a subject if an aide can do it for him? Just watch senators step out of the elevator on their way into the chamber for a vote. Many will quickly glance to the side where aides stand compressing into a single gesture the sum of information their bosses need: thumbs up or thumbs down.[9]

CONGRESSIONAL OVERLOAD

Congressional bureaucracy has become as much a reality as executive branch bureaucracy. Much of the time of the legislative bureaucracy is devoted to so-called "constituent service," acting as ombudsmen for a constituent who might be confronted with seemingly intractable problems with a department or agency. Ironically, Congress has generated this workload for itself over the years by having created the very departments, agencies, and programs with which it now must cope.

"There are now signs that the limits of capacity have been reached. . . . The enormous extension of the activities of the federal government generates a volume of detailed and complex business which I believe has gone beyond the capacity of Congress to handle. . . . A law of diminishing returns is actively at work in the field of the federal government. . . . The workload is beyond effective legislative control."[10] A lamentation of a member in the 1980s? No. Testimony on the legislative reorganization act in *1948*. Even then it was apparent to many that Washington was simply trying to do too much, that the federal government was out of control.

NO ONE IN CHARGE

The federal government has grown so large that no single individual can possibly comprehend it in any kind of detail. Even David Stockman, who most concede had an incredible grasp of the federal structure as Director of the Office of Management and Budget, only hit the "high spots." Senators and members of Congress will acknowledge that while they might master the governmental activities controlled by the committees on which they serve, it is impossible to be conversant with everything government does. *There is simply no one in charge*.

Since those whom we elect are overwhelmed, the non-elected take over. The bureaucrats and congressional staff really manage the government—and as often as not they do it *their way.* Once again government's size serves to obscure their transgressions.

"JACK OF ALL TRADES . . ."

Beyond the size of government *per se,* we have simply asked the federal government to do too many different kinds of things—and it is doing none of them well. The old saying, "Jack of all trades, master of none," fits government perfectly.

Those elected to the federal government must comprehend and administer all areas of human existence. As a result, the things which only the federal government can do—defense, foreign affairs, national security—suffer as our President and key congressional leaders spend their limited time on everything from roads to welfare to food stamps, student loans, sewer systems, anthropological studies, cancer research, air traffic control, weather prediction, land management, and dredging harbors, preserving Indian lore, building jet fighters, staffing embassies, preventing terrorism, protecting farmers, regulating stocks and bonds, controlling communications, putting up satellites, regulating highway speed, and determining the acceptable miles-per-gallon of our automobiles (this is only a tiny peek at the range of human concerns with which Washington deals). No group of human beings is that smart.

Congress tries to cope with this proliferation of responsibilities through committees and sub- committees, giving chairmen enormous powers. The committee system is a perfectly logical and manageable approach, so long as each legislator has a chance to assess and reflect upon the recommendations of the committee.

But when everyone is so "stretched" that the committee recommendations are not adequately tested and challenged, the nation's policy direction is determined largely by committees (and, increasingly, by their non-elected staffs) and by the chairmen who accede to power not by any particular measure of competence but primarily by seniority (and in the House, by the degree of loyalty exhibited toward the party). Those things which only the federal government can and must do compete for time and attention with things that states, local governments, and private individuals and organizations can (and should) do, leaving true national priorities to suffer.

CHAPTER 6

CURRENT POLITICAL REALITIES

> It is the highest impertinence and presumption . . . in kings and ministers, to pretend to watch over the economy of private people, and to restrain their expense, either by sumptuary laws, or by prohibiting the importation of foreign luxuries. They are themselves always, and without any exception, the greatest spendthrifts in the society. Let them look well after their own expenses, and they may safely entrust private people with theirs. If their own extravagance does not ruin the state, that of their subjects never will.
> (*Adam Smith*, The Wealth of Nations, *1776*)

WE have reviewed the facts regarding the expansion of the Congress itself as a reflection of the growth of government generally and, from the numbers, have some notion of why Washington is in such trouble. But only in part does that explain how we made the transition from a very limited to a virtually limitless federal structure that has driven taxes and spending to unprecedented levels.

The "rest of the story" is, I believe, to be found by analyzing how representation really works—the dynamic interaction between those whom we elect and those whom our elected officials really end up representing.

Once the engines of federal revenue were in place and

the potential for using government as an instrument for coercive social change became apparent, social engineers flocked to Washington.

SOCIAL ENGINEERS INVADE WASHINGTON

They created a blizzard of alphabet agencies in the 1930s, using the economic woes of the time as their justification, in turn exacerbating those woes. Their programs and agencies began as fragile children, some of whom died in infancy at the hands of an initially unfriendly Supreme Court. But as the judicial climate changed, many of the offspring grew to expensive adulthood.

Since those uneasy beginnings, new programs and agencies have proliferated like mushrooms in a dark cave. And each one has become more adroit at survival and expansion. Whether or not a program or agency accomplishes anything worthwhile, it builds a constituency for its perpetuation. To paraphrase Will Rogers' comment that "I never met a man I didn't like," government responds, "I never saw a program I didn't want to keep."

FOOD STAMPS—
POWER BEHIND A PROGRAM

An example of the development of a program that has enormous momentum is food stamps. Food stamps were first issued some 20 years ago. Before then they did not exist. There simply were no food stamps. The program started with a few million dollars and a handful of recipients; today food stamps are received by 18 million people (one out of every 14 people in the United States) and cost us nearly more than $12 billion a year.[1]

Has the food stamp program stamped out hunger? Not if you listen to advocates for the poor. By the government's measure of poverty, the portion of the population that is below the so-called poverty line today is not substantially different from 1967. Why then does such a program continue? Because there are so many interests with a stake in it, including *the members of the House and Senate* from farm states whose Agriculture Committees oversee the program; the Department of Agriculture's vast *bureacracy* that administers the program; the *suppliers* to the program—farmers, storage and transportation companies, the supermarket chains, the retail clerks union, the printing concerns that print the stamps, and so forth; the farm lobbyists, agriculture trade groups, and the social "public interest" groups; and the *recipients* of the stamps.

Think of the political "reach" of these interests. They are awesome. Despite many food stamp abuses, these interests have successfully resisted any significant reduction in the program.

SPECIAL INTERESTS FLOURISH

Over the years, the special interest groups have become increasingly professional and capable. They have become adept not only at carving a *piece* of the government pie, but at *increasing the size of the pie*. This is perfectly understandable. As more money has flowed to Washington to be spent, more able people have followed that money to influence how it is spent. One need only review the migration to Washington over the last half century of various business, trade, and other special interest organizations, as well as the proliferation of lobbyists and law firms, to know where the power in this country lies.

In 20 years, from 1966-86, business, trade, public-interest, and other such organizations have multiplied nationally from 2,000 to more than 6,300. During that same approximate time period, the number of such organizations headquartered in the District of Columbia has increased from fewer than 400 to nearly 2,000. Washington's share of these organizations grew from less than 19 percent of the total to 31 percent, while New York and other areas of the nation have experienced a decrease in the number of associations (only Chicago has held its own).[2]

Even these figures do not tell the whole story. Many organizations that maintain their principal headquarters outside of Washington have opened Washington offices or increased dramatically the size of existing Washington offices. National trade groups employ 80,000 people in Washington, making it the third largest industry after government and tourism. John Kelly, Communications Director of the Greater Washington Society of Association Executives, said, "in the last 15 years the role of associations has increasingly turned to lobbying the government. What better place to do it."[3]

"LOBBYING," BUREAUCRACY-STYLE

Lobbying is by no means restricted to those we call "lobbyists." Some of lobbying's finest practitioners are to be found within our bureaucracies.

We prefer to believe that federal departments and agencies are subject to the will of the President and Congress. If a program or department becomes outmoded, wasteful, duplicative, or just plain unnecessary, those whom we elect will get rid of it. Right? Hardly!

Bureaucracy has devised defense mechanisms that make pruning of government a very difficult task, indeed. The irony is that these defenses are paid for by us. Taxpayers' resources are employed to prevent the pruning.

The defense mechanisms of the bureaucracy can be broadly defined as "lobbying:" direct lobbying, semi-direct, indirect, and informal. Let's consider them:

• *DIRECT LOBBYING.* Despite the fact that federal law prohibits lobbying by federal employees, "legislative liaison" offices have emerged in every department and agency in order to "respond" to inquiries and requests from Congress. No one has been able to get a handle on the amount of money devoted to the salaries and activities of these offices, but clearly they amount to hundreds of millions of dollars.[4]

These lobbyists are among the most prolific and persuasive in Washington, often "outshooting" the hired-gun lobbyists in the private sector. These advocates present and defend the department and agency budgets and are often the source of new and expanded activities of their "employers." For, after all, everyone in government depends for his advancement, pay, and prestige on the number of employees and the size of the budget with which he has to work.

• *SEMI-DIRECT LOBBYING.* Taxpayer funds are often granted to advocacy organizations that engage in direct lobbying of Congress on behalf of activities of the department or agency.[5] These grants fund political conferences and grass roots organizational activities, which if successful will generate an increasing demand for the "services" of that department or agency, leading to an expansion of its budget. In the early days of the war on poverty, grants were often given to people to go door to door or to work in community centers to expand the base of people eligible for welfare, housing assistance, food stamps, and other taxpayer-provided programs. We have all heard advertisements for various government publications, urging us to write to Pueblo, Colorado, for copies. This only serves to expand the activities of the Government Printing Office. The euphemism for all this activity in government circles is "outreach." What it really means is using your money to communicate the availability of more of your money.

• *INDIRECT LOBBYING*. Increasingly, government employees are members of employee associations or unions. A portion of your tax dollar that flows to pay the salaries of government employees is passed through in the form of dues to organizations that lobby to increase the power and size of the federal government. Public employee unions are the fastest- growing unions in America, thanks to your tax dollars. The government-employee affiliates of the AFL-CIO and the other public employee unions lobby for a big-spending social welfare agenda and contribute heavily to the liberal, big-spending members of Congress who, in turn, seek to expand those activities which will create more dues-paying jobs.

The social worker organizations and the teachers organizations are all dependent for their power on a "pass-through" of taxes in the form of dues. When the poverty lawyers first came on the scene in the late 1960s and early

1970s, they saw a great opportunity to influence the mainstream legal profession. Using part of their taxpayer-provided salaries, the poverty lawyers paid dues to the National Legal Aid and Defenders Association (NLADA—part of the American Bar Association) and through sheer numbers took control of NLADA. Through it, they influenced the ABA to accept plaintiff solicitation and other case "manufacturing" techniques that had been considered unethical over the years.

• *INFORMAL LOBBYING.* In Washington, it is not at all uncommon that a wife might be a secretary in one department or agency and her husband a principal staff person for a House or Senate member. The mere proximity of all of the elements of the federal government assures a very high level of informal lobbying that, in many instances, is more effective than the work of those lobbyists who are registered or who populate the congressional liaison offices.

The bureaucracy's skill at protecting its interests through lobbying of all types has created a virtual perpetual-motion machine of departments and agencies in Washington.

THE "VENUS FLYTRAP"

Washington's seductive nature becomes evident when a newly-elected member of the House or Senate arrives in Washington. It can best be described as the "venus-flytrap" syndrome.

That new, fresh-faced congressman just in from America's heartland has promised his constituents he would stand tall against the alien big spenders in Washington. He is about to be given the "treatment." First, a group of deferential Hill staffers show him to his suite of offices which may well be the best he's ever occupied. The Air Force takes him on a "tour" of some of its facilities, sometimes referred to as a "junket;" lobbyists escort him to the Kennedy Center for a major musical production; foreign nations wine and dine him at embassy receptions on Massachusetts Avenue. Pretty soon home doesn't look nearly as glamorous as Washington. With the exception of a few mavericks, it is not long before the member succumbs and becomes Washington's ambassador back to his district.

Congress has become a full-time body, because most of the members would prefer to remain in Washington than go back and live with their constituents. In most instances they bring their wives and children, who quickly become Washingtonians. The trap has been sprung. They have been co-opted by the system.

CAREERIST MENTALITY

The legislators enjoy the power and perks and look forward to an incredibly generous pension. They don't want to give these up. They adopt a careerist mentality. They will do almost anything to get re- elected so they can stay in Washington. Best evidence of that is what they do when they leave Congress. A good many of them stay in Washington, adding to the throngs of lobbyists circling the Washington "light."

As Brutus warned us in 1787 regarding our Senators, they "will for the most part of the time be absent from the

MYTH

Government employees are public servants who seek to promote the good of the people.

REALITY

The federal government today is much more an omnipresent "big brother" than an "Uncle Sam." Washington is not a friendly relative. Just ask anyone who has "crossed" the IRS or tried to speed up a regulatory agency.

And the larger it has become, the more removed, faceless, independent, and unresponsive the federal government has grown. Government employees often treat the taxpayers who foot the bill as servants, not masters.

Government employees, through civil service protection, enjoy virtual lifetime tenure, irrespective of performance. They constitute a political force of ever-increasing proportions within the federal government itself. Through their public employee unions and associations, they heavily influence the salaries and benefits they receive, including retirement programs unmatched by those in the private sector. The very size and power of government itself is influenced by the lobbying, public relations, and media efforts of public employees fueled by taxpayer dollars.

state they represent, and associate with such company as will possess very little of the feelings of the middling class of people. *For it is to be remembered that there is to be a federal city, and the inhabitants of it will be the great and the mighty of the earth.*"[6]

GOODBYE STEWARDSHIP, HELLO "OWNERSHIP"

Another current political reality in Washington has to do with what can be termed "proprietary interests." Any Senator or member of the House who has been in Washington for a long time—or any new member who arrives in Washington with a careerist mentality—develops a sense of "ownership" over particular programs, departments, or agencies. Representative Claude Pepper, whose tenure in the House challenged the memory of the most ardent Washingtonphile, was a perfect example. He saw himself as the official watchdog of social security and other "senior" citizens' programs. Tip O'Neill exhibited a sense of "ownership" over the House of Representatives, as did Jim Wright, who evidently thought of himself as Secretary of State for Central America. Many Speakers have considered the House their own "private preserve." Committee chairmen often operate their committees as private fiefdoms.

Far from approaching congressional service as a fiduciary responsibility or a trust, too many long-standing members develop a proprietary interest or ownership interest in government. That enormous difference in outlook produces an equally enormous difference in outcome—an increasing propensity to expand government and expend more money in order to nurture that which they "own."

To many members, spending is their job. That's what they do for a living. Like a surgeon who never makes an incision, a legislator who doesn't spend is an anachronism in the eyes of liberal legislators. Most don't need to spend to be re-elected. They're "safe." But they spend anyway because spending is their only reason for existence.

The attitude of "proprietorship" is nurtured by the virtual lifetime tenure of many members of Congress. If House and Senate terms were limited, it is much more likely that "short timers" would retain a fiduciary rather than a proprietary outlook. (A proposal for term limitation is outlined in Chapter 13.)

CONGRESS THWARTS PRESIDENT'S FISCAL MANAGEMENT

A natural consequence of Congress's "proprietary" attitude has been the growing tendency for Congress to micromanage expenditures, denying the President the authority to set priorities and reduce spending. For example, under President Reagan, then- Secretary of Energy Don Hodel sought to maintain a lean work force, hoping to eliminate the Energy Department entirely. Congress ordered him to fill 300 to 400 positions that he had not requested in his departmental budget, did not want, and had no need for. Congress compelled him to hire people to fill the new "slots." Hodel did not want anyone to believe that these people were needed. Therefore, he ordered that his existing staff not share their work with the new employees. The new people sat at empty desks, with quiet telephones, having absolutely nothing to do. Hodel was trying to manage his operation, and Congress would not let him do it. Ronald Reagan urged the elimination of many agencies and programs in his budget proposals. He sought to rescind or defer expenditures of funds he felt were unnecessary and wasteful. He was willing to take the political "heat" personally for these actions. What did he get for his trouble? Rejection from Congress, which insisted that he keep right on spending.

GOVERNMENT IS NOT A BUSINESS

This points up one of the crucial misconceptions about government. Government is not like a business. It cannot be made business-like. The President is not a CEO. He cannot make policy and enforce it. He does not control the resources of the "company." Only the Congress can spend.

Congress has refused to give the President additional tools with which to control spending. It has denied him a line-item veto and has constrained the exercise of his traditional constitutionally- authorized veto power. In Fiscal Years 1987 and 1988 Congress approved and sent to the President (after the respective fiscal years had begun) huge omnibus spending bills—rather than the usual 13 major appropriations bills—essentially daring him to veto them and shut down much of government. These grab-bag spending monstrosities included billions for pork barrel projects of an entirely local nature. (In my judgment, the President should have vetoed the objectionable parts and dared Congress to challenge him in the courts. He might have established a "line-item veto" in that way.)

MYTH

Government can be made efficient if we would only run it like a business.

REALITY

Government is wholly *unlike* a business and can never be made to run like one.

By virtue of the separation of powers built into our Constitution, the "buck" does not stop in any particular place. There is no Chief Executive Officer in the same sense as in a corporation. The President cannot make policy and enforce it. Congress controls spending and uses that power to influence policy, both by withholding funds and by forcing the expenditure of funds on programs to which the President objects. Congress has no true "institutional" responsibility. The primary interest of the 100 Senators and 435 Representatives is re-election. Making government work is only marginally related to re-election.

While a businessman has to satisfy his customers to enjoy a flow of cash, agency heads who get their funding from Congress (their customer) need not satisfy the people to survive. As a monopoly supplier, without competition in most of the things it does, government responds as one would expect—slowly and inefficiently. That's the way it is. The only way to reduce inefficiency in government is to reduce government.

"GERRYMANDERING"—
INCUMBENT INSURANCE

In our frustration over Congress's inability to discipline itself, many yearn to "throw the rascals out and elect a new team." Gerrymandering (drawing congressional district lines for the benefit of an incumbent) used to be just an "art." With the advent of sophisticated computers and voter profiles, gerrymandering has become a "science." Districts have been made so safe that an incumbent is virtually assured of re-election unless he molests little children publicly. Even admitted homosexuals have been returned to Congress in some districts. (Incumbents of the minority party have demonstrated their willingness to approve redistricting plans that guarantee the majority party an excessive preponderance of the seats, so long as the minority incumbents' seats remain "safe" for them.)

Walter Dean Burnham, Professor of Political Science at MIT, observed recently: "Incumbent protection at the polls produced a 1986 House election that was structurally the most uncompetitive since 1832. Only one Democrat and five Republican incumbents lost. Congressional winners outside the South got at least 60 percent of their district vote in four-fifths of the districts, and this, too, was an all-time record. Assisted by the tremendous advantages House incumbents now have in cash and visibility, House elections are well on their way to becoming frozen in concrete."[7]

In the 1988 congressional races, the result was equally grim. Only four districts in which incumbents sought re-election changed hands—just a one percent turnover. Washington lawyer Robert L. Corn notes that this phenomenon of invulnerable incumbents ". . . contrasts sharply with the record of congressional turnover in the 19th and the early 20th centuries, when it was common for 40 to 50 percent of the incumbents to be replaced. Even as late as the first third of this century the *average* House turnover ranged from one-fourth to one-third of the total membership. Such large turnovers are unlikely to recur, given the institutionalization of incumbency benefits."[8]

In addition to the gerrymandering advantage, incumbent congressmen have postage-free newsletters to their districts, expansive staffs, high media visibility. A challenger would have to spend over a million dollars just to achieve the name recognition and exposure the incumbent develops free through mailings, in-district staff, etc.[9]

As things stand today, reforming Washington by electing a different cast in the House is a forlorn hope, *unless* the composition of key state legislatures is changed in the elections of 1990. Then congressional redistricting could affect the House in the elections of 1992.

"INSIDE-THE-BELTWAY" LINGO

Another very important aspect of the current political reality is the "inside-the-beltway" mentality (the "beltway" runs through Maryland and Virginia circling the nation's capital). One manifestation of this mentality is the use of the English language. Winston Churchill once said that England and America are the only two nations in history separated by a common language. That is now equally true as between Washington and the rest of America. Recently, former Secretary of Labor Bill Brock quipped, "Competitiveness is the new code word in

Washington, and Washington needs code words. It doesn't think in sentences very often."[10]

SPENDING "CUTS"

Over the years Washington has developed its own fiscal language that amounts to a foreign tongue anywhere outside the capital beltway. It uses this language when discussing spending and taxing in order to soften the blow on the poor taxpayer. Take the innocent phrase, "*spending cuts.*" That means reductions in federal spending, right? Wrong. Not even close. The word "cut" is used differently in Washington than it is anywhere else. In the language of government, a cut is a reduction in the projected growth rate of spending. In other words, if a given program is expected to mushroom at 10 percent a year, and if by some miracle of congressional restraint it expands only eight percent, it has been "cut."

Such language is intended to deceive us long-suffering taxpayers back home. The program hasn't been cut. It is still growing like a toadstool on a rotten log. While the media selectively feature "those heartless spending cuts," overall federal spending has remained at a peacetime record percentage of the GNP.

The only reason the liberals can get away with this linguistic sleight-of-hand is because the federal government uses what is called a "current services" budget. That is, each year's budget is automatically increased the next year for cost-of-living increases and new entrants. Therefore, any reduction in the automatic increase is referred to as a "cut." By adopting "baseline" budgeting, which uses the prior year's actual spending as the baseline, you do not succumb to the liberals' rules of the budgetary game.

"TAX EXPENDITURES"

One of the most frightening phrases is "tax expenditure." It is used by the politicians and bureaucrats to describe a provision of the tax code which enables *you* to retain part of what *you* earn. What it indicates is a Washington state of mind that everything you earn belongs to the government, but that by government's grace you get to keep something. That which you retain is as much an "expenditure" of taxes as government's purchase of a missile or payment of the salary of a federal judge. It is "newspeak" reminiscent of Orwell's *1984*.

FROM "DOLE" TO "ENTITLEMENT"

"Entitlements" and "automatics" are among the most repugnant of Washington's lexicon. No longer do we provide "assistance" to those "down on their luck," we owe them sustenance; hence, they are "entitled" to be supported. And the benefits are automatically adjusted by statute for inflation or other changes so that Congress can duck the responsibility of having to vote on them. Congress has put much of the budget on automatic pilot so it can claim that increases are out of its hands.

A TAX INCREASE BY ANY OTHER NAME

Increasing taxes is less painful to many politicians than cutting spending. But our lawmakers recognizing that talking openly about a tax increase can be risky. So one must be sensitive to new words and phrases that may be euphemisms for "tax increase." "Revenue enhancement" looked like a good try recently, but it was pretty transparent. In 1984, when they told us they were making a "down payment on the deficit," that was a new one. Only later did we find that the size of the tax increase was exceeded by the amount of additional spending.

In short, whenever those inside the beltway say anything at all about taxes, rates, revenues, or the like, however innocent it sounds, set off the alarms and hide your cash. They are not in this to enhance your revenue or to reduce the deficit, but to corral more spendable cash for *their* pet political projects.

With so much rigging of the political vocabulary, it is a wonder that those outside the beltway can unravel the fiscal mysteries of Washington at all.

•

In the 1986 and the 1988 elections, tens of millions of eligible voters stayed away from the polls. Could this be a signal that, unable to comprehend the size and complexities of Washington, citizens are tuning government out— that popular control over the federal government has waned, enabling those who are supposed to serve the public to become its masters? There is the unsettling feeling across America that the inmates are running the asylum.

MYTH

Finally, Congress is getting serious and is "cutting" spending.

REALITY

Congress is doing nothing of the kind. Total spending continues to increase. In Washington, "cut" doesn't mean what it does in Peoria, Kalamazoo, or Tucson. In bureaucratise, "cut" means "slow the rate of growth." So, if Congress keeps a program from its usual explosive growth rate, that's a "cut," and a victory for "newspeak," Washington style.

PART III

WE'VE REACHED THE LIMIT

CHAPTER 7

THE REDISTRIBUTION GAME

Sometimes the law defends plunder and participates in it. Thus the beneficiaries are spared the shame and danger that their acts would otherwise involve. . . .

But how is this legal plunder to be identified? Quite simply. See if the law takes from some persons what belongs to them and gives it to the other persons to whom it doesn't belong. *See if the law benefits one citizen at the expense of another by doing what the citizen himself cannot do without committing a crime.*

Then abolish that law without delay. For it is not only an evil in itself but also a fertile source for further evils because it invites reprisals and imitation. If such a law—which may not be an isolated case—is not abolished immediately, it will spread, multiply and develop into a system. . . .

No legal plunder; this is the principle of justice, peace, order, stability, harmony and logic.

(*Emphasis added.*)
(*Frederick Bastiat,* The Law,*1850*)

IT'S one thing to maintain our nation's defenses, to keep the federal courts open, and to preserve our national monuments and national parks. Generally speaking, we all derive benefit from these activities of the federal government. Economists like to call these "public goods"—governmental activities the benefits of which are shared equally by all taxpayers.

No one can deny that the defense provided by our armed services is a benefit to each and every American who, as a result, remains free from subjugation by the nation's enemies. We might argue about the total amount expended or whether it is spent wisely, but national defense and other public goods benefit us all.

Unfortunately, a very large portion of federal spending conveys only private benefits. Everyone has gotten into the act. Programs for the poor represent only part of this redistribution scheme. Those in the middle- and upper-income groups receive generous subsidies, too. Here are some examples of federal programs that have little, if anything, to do with poor people:

• *AMTRAK*. Amtrak benefits an easily definable class—those who ride it. The annual subsidy to Amtrak users is $33 per person. On the eastern seaboard of the United States, that subsidy serves commuters whose average income is well over $30,000 a year.

• *FARM SUBSIDIES*. Taxpayers everywhere, including other farmers and ranchers who are not subsidized, are taxed and those funds redistributed to a select group of people engaged in the production of wheat, corn, cotton, and a handful of other crops. And for what? To not produce or to overproduce so we must transport and store their products, artificially raising the prices we pay—so we pay twice. It encourages the government to dump our commodities abroad where they destroy local agriculture that we are at the same time trying to improve by funding Peace Corps volunteers.

Milton Friedman has observed that in the 19th century when more than half our population lived on farms, farmers would never have dreamed of farm price supports. They would have had to tax themselves to pay themselves subsidies. Now that they constitute only a tiny fraction of our population, farmers—and their representatives in Congress—can benefit mightily from the U.S. Treasury while paying only a small part of the bill.

And yet many farmers—those who are good businessmen, control their debt structure and employ up-to-date, scientific agricultural techniques—want an end to subsidies and government interference in agriculture. They recognize the kind of perverse results that the current system encourages. For example:

The government's Byzantine system of wasteful subsidies encourages some people to become farmers just so they can "farm the government," writes Mitzi Ayala, President-Elect of American Agri Women. Speaking from personal experience as a rice grower in Davis, California, Miss Ayala continued, "Since someone figured out a way to take advantage of the rice-subsidy system last year, the number of rice growers in my county has grown to 72 from 50. They are not planting rice because Americans suddenly have discovered a passion for Rice-A-Roni."

To understand why subsidies have created more rice farmers, consider the hypothetical example of "Farmer Brown." Farmer Brown owns a 2,000-acre parcel of rice land, slightly more than double the size of the average California rice farm. Under the rice-subsidy program, which was set up to protect small farms, his maximum payment is $50,000 a year. Farmer Brown knows exactly how many acres of rice to plant to reach that limit, roughly 200. Any rice he plants beyond the 200 acres will not be profitable.

Does that mean that he takes his remaining 1,800 acres out of rice production? Not at all. Instead, he rents 200 acres each to nine others, who grow just enough rice to get their maximum $50,000 payments in government subsidies. These nine other farmers probably never grew rice before, and they certainly would not be doing so now if it weren't for the subsidies.[1]

And if you think of farm subsidies in terms of saving the small farmer who is pictured on television losing his farm and equipment at a bankruptcy auction, think again. In an editorial, "Paying Edison Not to Grow Corn," *The Chicago Tribune* noted that "Congress has been unable to fine-tune the system to prevent large payments to wealthy farmers."

Commonwealth Edison leases 33,000 acres of its farmland surrounding its generating facilities in northern Illinois. Edison's 1986 subsidy was scheduled at $540,000, and the farmers who lease the land from Edison are subsidized to the tune of $1.3 million. Travelers Insurance of Hartford, Connecticut, was also in line for $340,000 of your tax dollars delivered in the form of farm subsidies through the U.S. Department of Agriculture.[2]

If ever there was justification for the redistribution game known as farm subsidies, it has long since evaporated. If the federal government had never tampered with agriculture, an orderly attrition of farmers would have taken place year by year. That's what has happened in the beef cattle industry which is not subsidized. The less efficient producers got out of the business, and those remaining have had to adjust to changes in America's eating habits. That is the way it should be.

• *STUDENT LOANS*. What was launched under the guise of giving students from poor families a chance for a college education has become a multi-billion dollar boondoggle that provides loans to students of all economic levels.

There have been so many defaults that it might as well have been an outright grant program from the beginning. Of the current outstanding loans of $12 billion, nearly half are in default; and, in 1986, at 115 schools, every student defaulted on his first payment.[3]

• *SCHOOL LUNCHES*. Initially intended to assist poor children in meeting minimum nutrition standards, this multi-billion dollar program serves nearly four billion lunches to children of all income groups, with a menu determined less by nutritionists than by lobbyists for various food producers vying to unload their surplus commodities at advantageous prices. From Alaska comes pressure to include tuna and salmon cakes. California lobbies to include raisins and canned apricots. Michigan cherry growers push cherries. From the dairy industry, which generally cranks out enormous surpluses, comes heavy pressure to purchase its products. As a result, disproportionate amounts of dairy goods, containing animal fats and cholesterol, find their way onto the school lunch trays.[4]

• *DEFENSE PROGRAMS*. Congress's redistributional propensities are not confined to civilian life. Senators and Representatives work hard to get defense contracts for their constituents. High-priced toilet seats, hammers, screws, etc., are the result.

Some time ago the Air Force decided it did not need any more T-46 trainer aircraft. The contractor for the craft, Fairchild Industries, happened to manufacture the T-46 in the Long Island, New York, district of the late chairman of a powerful House defense committee. The chairman, and others in the New York delegation, insisted that more T-46s be included in the Air Force budget.[5]

Prime defense contractors regularly seek out subcontractors in as many congressional districts as possible to increase the political clout they can generate at the time major contracts are awarded.

MILITARY BASE BOONDOGGLE

When the Department of Defense seeks to eliminate a domestic military installation, in order to reduce duplication and free up funds for higher priority items, it runs into a political buzzsaw. On the Hill, Senators and Representatives who may be totally anti-defense nevertheless rally to preserve "that critically important installation" in their state or district. To hear them talk you would think their installation is the only thing standing between the United States and a Soviet takeover.

At a time when the federal budget is being tightened because of huge deficits, and the military budget is in for special assault, the military simply must be given the freedom and flexibility to manage resources effectively. Recently, Edward H. Crane, President of the Cato Institute, reported that "while a Pentagon study showed we needed about 312 military bases throughout the world, we have, in fact, 3,868 in the United States alone."[6] We simply must reduce this stunning array of separate facilities, consolidating some functions and reducing overhead.

In the waning days of the 100th Congress, a base-closing bill authored by fiscal watchdog Congressman Dick Armey (R-TX) was passed by Congress. It empowers a non-partisan commission to make base closing recommendations. Recently, many military installations around the nation were targeted for closure by the newly appointed commission. A PR firestorm has ensued. But this time the commission's recommendations will control the outcome unless—*unless*—Congress votes to block all base closures recommended by the commission. Maybe the new rules will frustrate Congress's propensity to use the defense budget for pork barreling. *But the big spenders in Congress should not be counted out yet.* If the commission's recommendations become law, Congress must make an initial appropriation to pay for the costs of closing the military bases. Should Congress refuse to pass such an appropriation, in whole or in part, it could frustrate the process. We'll have to wait and see.

•

The main beneficiaries of the great redistribution game are the "traffic cops" in Washington who handle the money and direct its use. Think of them as brokers. Bureaucracy gets an administrative fee. Legislators get a political "finder's fee" (re-election commitments, campaign funds, etc.).

Politicians derive their power and ensure their political futures by providing special benefits to some at the expense of the general taxpayer. Congress has created a web of redistribution that is a politician's delight and a taxpayer's nightmare. As the saying goes, "we are taking in each other's wash." Federal taxes taken from Californians are used to fill potholes on New York expressways; New Yorkers are taxed to build a waterway in Tennessee; from the Volunteer State federal tax funds flow to California to build a subway under Los Angeles's glittering Wilshire Boulevard (hardly poverty row). If these projects are meritorious, let those who will benefit pay for them directly. It is ludicrous to route our tax dollars through Washington: "A system that increasingly has Congress, in effect, buying the support of voters with their own money is self-destructive and, frankly, ignoble."[7]

The sense that dollars are "free" because they come from Washington merely serves to intensify the pressure for spending because there is no direct, immediate, related, and focused "pain" of taxes to provide a countervailing force to the "pleasure" of spending. But the politicians who divide this pie love it.

Their interest is in increasing the size of that pie so there is more to divvy up. Though redistribution is their game, it shouldn't be ours, because it is a cornerstone of spendthrift government and a source of enormous unfairness in our nation, underlying much of our national discontent.

MYTH

We've cut federal spending "to the bone."

REALITY

Federal spending could and should be cut by billions. The Grace Commission findings, Heritage Foundation studies, an earlier review by the National Tax Limitation Committee, all confirm that billions are wasted on: duplicative military bases and facilities; social research studies; grants for poets and local theater groups; counter-productive farm subsidies; wasteful contracting procedures; student loans to children in well-to-do families; purely local roads, sewer systems, and other projects financed by the federal government. The list is endless.

When a politician says spending has been "cut to the bone," what he is really saying is that he can't muster the political will to make hard decisions on spending cuts, or that he likes to spend your money to provide benefits to those who can assure his re-election.

CHAPTER 8

REDISTRIBUTION BY "CRISIS"

Hooray, a Drought—America's farmers may be praying for rain, but in Washington they're breaking out another kind of liquid refresher—champagne. There's nothing like a little hardship to justify more spending and self congratulation. Here's to you, pain and suffering.

(The Wall Street Journal)[1]

WITH public scrutiny beginning, just beginning, to blunt runaway redistribution, *new* federal programs are tougher to justify. Congress has come to rely on "crises" to rationalize new spending. But there is always competition in meeting crises, because many private individuals and institutions are ready and willing to help. The "thousand points of light," as President Bush calls them, include the Red Cross, Rotary International, Jerry Lewis' telethon, churches, foundations, and many others.

Members of Congress want to be "heroes," and to enjoy the political payoff of heroism, by spending other people's money. Washington is always striving to become a "sole-source supplier" of crisis solutions, trying to take advantage of some hot or visible issue of the moment.

As we consider each of these "crises," try to remember how they were hyped to get your attention and how they were assigned "apple-pie-and-motherhood" names designed to intimidate congressional opponents. Let's start with the drought itself.

• *DROUGHT RELIEF.* As is almost universally true, a particular problem is solved about the time Congress gets around to addressing it. The rains came as Congress deliberated. But the momentum was already there. Senate Agricultural Committee Chairman Pat Leahy, from the dairy farm state of Vermont, used the opportunity of the drought to provide the dairy industry with additional goodies from the public treasury.

Then the other farm state Senators and Representatives, using the drought "crisis" as justification for wide-ranging mischief, dusted off pet projects that had been sitting on the shelf awaiting just such an occasion: more subsidies to corn growers to produce ethanol at prices far exceeding the pump price of gasoline; export subsidies for sunflower and cottonseed oil; and on and on.[2]

Billions of dollars later, our heroes take their bows and step back to admire how effectively they met that crisis— by another massive redistribution of other people's money.

• *THE CLEAN WATER ACT AMENDMENTS.* In the fall of 1986, Congress passed a whopping $18 billion spending bill that it labeled the Clean Water Act. And who can object to clean water? We just had to have this massive cleanup of our water—or we might perish.

But a look at the bill revealed it was almost entirely devoted to funding *local* sewer projects.[3] Why in the world is the federal government involved in something as uniquely local as sewage treatment, you ask, especially when many state and local governments have a budget surplus and the federal government has a huge budget deficit? If the bill had been called the "Sewage Treatment Bill," opponents of this kind of pork barrel might have had the courage to oppose it head on. Label it "The Clean Water Act" and you intimidate the opposition.

President Reagan "pocket" vetoed the bill, only to have Congress pass it again as its first action of the 100th Congress. The President vetoed it again, citing its budget-busting, Gramm-Rudman-Hollings-violating character, but his veto was overridden. So much for congressional belt tightening.

• *INFRASTRUCTURE*. Remember a few years back when we were told our roads were about to disintegrate and our bridges collapse? Congress rushed to pass a massive public works bill and tacked on a hefty gasoline tax to pay for it. Every legislator's pet project for his state or district that had been on his "rainy-day" list was tucked into this spending monstrosity. Media hype carried the day. Who can be for a crumbling "infrastructure"—that would be tantamount to approving of fallen arches. Only a chronic Scrooge could oppose such spending.

• *THE WAR ON DRUGS*. Late in 1986, everyone jumped into the drug battle. The President and Mrs. Reagan led the fight. "Just say no" was the watchword. Congress was delighted—another new spending opportunity. Commenting on the $6 billion bill passed by Congress, Citizens for a Sound Economy (CSE), a Washington-based public policy think tank, reported:

The vast majority of the money appropriated is unlikely to have any effect on the problem of individual drug abuse. Rep. Barney Frank (D-MA) remarked, "I fear this bill is the legislative equivalent of crack. It yields a short-term high, but does long-term damage to the system and it's expensive to boot." Congress has exploited a politically sensitive issue to create pork-barrel programs that will generate patronage jobs and public works spending in home districts, while doing little to genuinely relieve the plight of those who abuse drugs.

Rep. William Hughes (D-NJ) stated the amendment "proposes too much money, too quickly for intelligent spending, with too little contribution by the recipient units of government . . . these moneys which were to be directed to drug enforcement are going to be siphoned off into prison construction at the state level."

One provision of HR 5484 authorizes spending $650,000 for a commission to study college athletic programs. The National Collegiate Athletic Association (NCAA) wrote that the measure "is in major part simply repetitive of ongoing initiatives already undertaken in the education community. Under these circumstances expenditure of $650,000 in taxpayer funds appear unwarranted.

CSE concluded: "The true problem resides in Congress: It is addicted to spending. The measure is just another opportunity for politicians to increase spending. If Congress wants to kick its spending habit, it should just say NO."[4]

• *SUPERFUND TOXIC WASTE CLEANUP.* Nothing gets the heart beating faster than visions of noxious, deadly chemicals and gases oozing and bubbling out of the ground, polluting the air and threatening groundwater. That's just what Congress was counting on when it passed the $9 billion superfund re-authorization bill in the fall of 1986. Here's what a Heritage Foundation research report revealed:

Although its defenders try to represent the Superfund re-authorization as a decisive action by Congress to address a matter of urgent national importance, the legislation is in fact one of the worst examples of budget-busting pork barrel politics in recent history. And in their haste to create this lucrative source of local public works projects, lawmakers have also established a whole new category of business "surtaxes" designed to raise over $2.7 billion, and a further $2.75 billion in taxes on the hard-pressed petroleum industry.

[T]he proponents of the legislation give the impression that the whole country is awash with dangerous chemicals, dumped by unknown polluters. In fact, in most instances the parties responsible for the hazardous wastes are known, and can be required to spend their own money to ensure that the wastes do not leak into the environment—in accordance with the "polluter pay" principle.

The Environmental Protection Agency has testified before Congress that it could not efficiently spend the money Congress wants to give it.

The pork barrel nature of the legislation is enhanced by the vague definitions it employs in determining just which sites would qualify for Superfund financing . . . any state or local government wishing to avoid the costs of finding a polluter or of cleaning up a local dumpsite would have the incentive simply to declare the dump an "abandoned hazardous waste site" and lay claim to "free" federal money.[5]

• *EMERGENCY JOBS PROGRAM.* In 1982-83, America was feeling the effects of recession and unemployment. Congress, always ready to respond—tardily—to any crisis, fashioned the 1983 Emergency Jobs Appropriations Act, using it as a convenient excuse for more pure political pork barreling. The General Accounting Office (GAO) investigated the results of this $9 billion program and issued a report. The GAO discovered that the law was passed two months *after* the jobless rate peaked at 11.4 percent; that 15 months after its passage, the program had created 35,000 jobs at a cost of $88,571 per job, while the private economy created 5,800,000 new jobs at no cost to the taxpayer (bringing the unemployment rate down to 7.4 percent); that 86 percent of the $9 billion was earmarked for *long-term* public works programs such as dams, airports, highways, and other pork-barrel programs, passed under the guise of the emergency need for jobs; and that the states with the worst unemployment problems got the least money per capita.[6]

Congress's timing led to public works spending during a period of rapid recovery and expansion, not recession, risking overheating the economy. But to Congress, redistribution is good anytime. And these projects serve two of the liberal big spenders' key political constituencies simultaneously: the public employee unions whose members are the bureaucrats who administer the projects; and the private sector unions whose members, in building the projects, are assured of the federal-government imposed "prevailing (union) wage."

• *EMERGENCY SUPPLEMENTAL APPROPRIATIONS BILL.* Citing impending disaster for the farmers unless the Commodity Credit Corporation's coffers were beefed up, the Senate in May 1987 passed an emergency bill. Having created a convenient spending vehicle with plenty of political momentum, the members of the Senate Appropriations Committee couldn't resist adding a few little goodies for special friends back home.

- North Dakota Democrat Quentin N. Burdick pushed an $8 million weed science center and a $600,000 farmer scholarship pilot program for North Dakota State University.

- Democrat Ernest F. Hollings swung $11.8 million to buy acreage for the Congaree Swamp refuge in his native South Carolina.

- Democrat Daniel K. Inouye won $200,000 for more staffing at Hawaii's Tern Island National Wildlife Refuge and $200,000 for a culture and arts development program.

- [Committee] Chairman . . . Mississippi Democrat John C. Stennis tacked on a provision that all future Strategic Defense Initiative testing be done at NASA sites, including the one in Mississippi's Hancock County.[7]

- *HOMELESSNESS.* Generations of Americans have known of hobos, nomads, tent cities, people who sleep in their cars, and those who traditionally have populated the "skid rows" of a thousand United States cities and towns. Only in the last several years has the term "homeless" been used in an intensive national PR campaign to create a new "crisis" to which Congress could be called upon to respond.

Through the Salvation Army, local churches, local-government-operated shelters, National Guard armories, and the like, almost no one who actually seeks shelter will be without it. The young mother with small children will *not* have to sleep on the street, under a bridge, or in a camp by the rails.

Advocates for the homeless in Chicago—"Chicago Coalition for the Homeless" (part of the National Coalition for the Homeless)—contended that Chicago's homeless numbered some 20,000 to 25,000. A rigorous, "on-the-ground" survey was conducted by Peter H. Rossi, sociology professor at University of Massachusetts, past president of the American Sociological Association and a self-proclaimed liberal. His research teams scoured Chicago from midnight to 6:00 a.m. over two separate two-week periods (in November and March), locating and interviewing people sleeping in all of Chicago's shelters, as well as in doorways, train stations, hospital waiting rooms, and elsewhere. He also adjusted for those who might have been on the streets but were temporarily housed in jail, in a hospital, or in prison.

HOMELESS NUMBERS VASTLY OVERSTATED

Rossi counted 2,722 homeless—a far cry from the 20,000 to 25,000 claimed by homeless advocates—and "we found no homeless children in our street searches."[8]

Rossi noted: "There have been other attempts to estimate the number of homeless persons in several cities. This generalization holds: *the more rigorous the attempt, the more likely it is that the resulting estimates of the homeless population are far smaller than those asserted by local advocacy communities.*"[9] (Emphasis added.)

Recently, in Los Angeles, where it is claimed that some 30,000 are homeless, tents were erected in a secure area and meals served by the Salvation Army under contract with the city. On the first day about 60 people showed up—only 25 or so of whom stayed overnight, although the 12-acre plot could hold many, many more. Some from nearby skid row vowed not to go to the facility. One was quoted as saying, "It's a circus, a freak show. I want to be out on my own. I don't want to be in no concentration camp. That's what it looks like." He was expressing the sentiments of many counted as homeless who prefer their *free* lifestyle.

Rossi's Chicago study and the Los Angeles experience should have been greeted with a sigh of relief by those who claim to speak for the homeless. They should have said, "Thank God the situation is not nearly so bad as we had believed." Instead, they have pilloried Rossi and shunned him unmercifully, treating him as a traitor.

"HOMELESSNESS" AS A POLITICAL WEAPON

The only explanation for this reaction is that "homelessness" is really not about shelter or housing. It is a weapon in an ideological war. For advocates of the homeless, homelessness represents a failure of the free enterprise system. The homeless are a "class" in a "class struggle." "The homeless are indeed the most egregious symbol of a cruel economy, an unresponsive government, a festering value system," claims Robert Hayes, leader of the National Coalition for the Homeless.[10] Homeless advocates often refer to the poor as "victims" or as being "victimized." Mitch Snyder, homeless guru and former adman, has said, "Homeless people are not responsible for their state. Like any oppressed people they need to fight."[11] Oppressed by whom? By our society, of course. The "victims" are not blamed for their own condition and they are not asked to do anything to overcome it.

When free shelter and food—instead of a cash grant—

is offered in a dormitory setting, it is rejected by those who claim to speak for the homeless as a "mandatory poorhouse" program.[12] This is a philosophy alien to the working, taxpaying citizens who are asked to foot the bill.

CONGRESS LEAPS BEFORE IT LOOKS

Not to be left on the PR sidelines or miss a golden opportunity for more spending, Congress has leapt into the fray. Without any competent evidence as to how many homeless there actually are (people who really want shelter and can't find it), Congress passed a $500 million "Urgent Relief for the Homeless Act" in early 1987. The funds were directed to the same agencies—HUD, HHS, etc.— that already had millions for these purposes. It appears that in 1986 there were at least 20 programs and $170-$200 million targeted for the "homeless" on top of regular welfare programs.[13]

The 1987 $500 million homeless act contained language that allowed funds to be used to demonstrate and lobby on behalf of the homeless.[14] We have been seeing evidence of these funds. It's hard to pick up a newspaper without seeing some story about homelessness. Taxpayer funds are being used to trumpet the need for more taxpayer funds. And the music goes round and round . . .

Lest we be accused of heartlessness, and making light of others' misfortune, be assured that no one who really wants shelter ought to be denied it. And they aren't. Shelters provided by churches, the Salvation Army and similar organizations, local governments, and private individuals abound.

On the coldest nights National Guard armories are opened. They are rarely filled—and yet we know that some people remain out of doors by choice. Why? Who are these people?

"HOMELESSNESS" IS NOT A HOUSING PROBLEM

When Sacramento County tried to profile the "average homeless," the best they could come up with was "male, 39, and caucasian."[15] This is probably a pretty good definition of the usual transient, but it doesn't get inside the problem. David Whitman, an associate editor of *U.S. News & World Report,* estimates that two-thirds of the homeless are mentally ill, drug addicts, or alcoholics, with some overlapping, of course.[16]

Columnist Charles Krauthammer links the advent of the homeless mentally ill with "the community mental health revolution" launched by President Kennedy in 1963 which "emptied America's state mental hospitals." In 1955 there were 559,000 mental patients; today there are 130,000, a decline of 75 percent.[17] These people were not cured, just released, and many were simply abandoned. So the federal government, as usual, precipitated the problem it now proposes to cure.

To make matters worse, the ACLU and others of a similar mind launched a legal crusade to prevent "involuntary hospitalization" of mental patients, further accelerating their disgorgement from asylums. "Today you can intervene to help the homeless mentally ill *only* if you can prove that *they are dangerous to themselves or to others.*

That standard is not just unfeeling, it is uncivilized. The standard should not be dangerousness but *helplessness*," urges Krauthammer.[18] (Emphasis added.)

HELPLESSNESS, NOT HOMELESSNESS

It is the helplessness of the mentally ill, not a lack of housing or shelter, that leads to their homelessness. It is simply not a homeless or even a shelter issue for the mentally ill. More public housing isn't the answer. Institutional care is. The same holds true for many transients whose lives and judgment have been shattered by alcohol and drugs.

Advocates for the homeless single out the Reagan administration for special blame, claiming it slashed the low-income housing budget and created a homeless problem. That is inaccurate. Not only have housing subsidies to low-income households risen from $5.7 billion in 1980 to $13.8 billion in 1988 (keeping ahead of the inflation rate), but more "bang for the buck" has been achieved through the use of housing vouchers. Renters are able to choose private units in the marketplace. Less reliance has been placed on expensive public housing.[19]

GOVERNMENT POLICIES AT THE HEART OF THE PROBLEM

But the federal government has once again been guilty of helping to create the problem it now seeks to solve. By handing out billions to local redevelopment agencies, it has prompted the demolition of many old core-city hotels and apartment houses which were the low-cost accommodations of transients, poor seniors, and others living on the margin. [20] Comparable alternative housing has rarely been provided.

Wherever local government has imposed rent control, as in New York City, the low-income housing shortage has been exacerbated. It is said that in New York more apartment units stand empty, gutted, and abandoned by their owners because of rent control than would be needed to house all those currently occupying shelters, welfare hotels, and the like. Instead, federal taxpayers subsidize half the $1800 or more monthly rent for one person in a New York welfare hotel. Where there's good money to be made providing hotel rooms for the homeless, you can be sure some real estate entrepreneur will turn homelessness into a very profitable business.

To the extent there are people without regular shelter, they are a local problem, not a national "crisis." The nature and size of the problem varies from area to area. January in Minneapolis poses a very different challenge than it does in Miami. Local leaders understand *their* problems far better than anyone in Washington. The only homeless problem with which Congress ought to concern itself is the one in Washington, D.C., because Congress has final authority over the operations of the nation's Capitol. It's doing a lousy job there. Why would we expect it to do better in Kalamazoo or Kankakee?

•

Government by crisis has proven outrageously expensive and wasteful. It has led to a further concentration of economic and political power in Washington; hasty, ill-conceived solutions that create as many (or more) problems as they solve; and political payoffs and naked redistribution, all of which frequently undermine the values of the taxpayers who pick up the tab.

Homelessness, crumbling infrastructure, and sewage and toxic waste disposal problems are intrinsically *local*, not *national* problems. Washington is too remote to be able to comprehend the details. At the local level, private as well as government resources can be mobilized effectively—and usually at a fraction of the cost. It is much tougher to convince local people familiar with the details that there is a *crisis* that justifies spending money without accountability. It is time to get Washington out of the "crisis" business.

CHAPTER 9

STEALING FROM OUR FUTURE

> Governments sometimes do the right thing, but only after they've exhausted all the alternatives.
>
> (*Anonymous*)

THOSE of us who have served in the military or in other branches of government know from firsthand experience that government is wasteful and inefficient. You put a lot in one end of the pipeline and don't get much out the other. We suspect this has had an adverse effect on the country and the growth of our economy.

But we don't have to rely on intuition. Recently, both the Rand Corporation and the World Bank completed studies on the effect that taxes and government spending have on economic growth. Independently, each concluded that big government means slower economic growth, which, of course, results in less wealth and lower-paying jobs.[1]

The Rand study found that for every 10 percent of a nation's total annual income that is taxed and spent by its government, the average growth rate of that nation's economy is reduced by one percent annually.[2] One percent per year might not sound like much, but its impact can be enormous.

Assume that the United States were to reduce the

proportion of its spending at all levels of government from 40 percent of our Gross Domestic Product (GDP) to about 20 percent. Assuming a current average annual real economic growth of about two percent, we would *double* the average annual rate of growth of our nation's economy— and *compound* that every year.

THE COMPOUNDING EFFECT

Using the accompanying chart, let's consider the impact on America, starting with an estimated FY-1987 GDP of $4.3 trillion ($4,359,000,000,000). You can see how dramatically the per-capita share of GDP increases in even 10 years as between an economy growing at two percent compounded versus four percent compounded. But the compounding effect over a generation of higher growth is truly astounding. At four percent compounded growth, the income per person in 25 years would be $39,239, nearly $15,000 more than would be produced at two percent compounded.

Nothing the federal government could do by way of job training, welfare, or unemployment insurance offers the same potential for the financial well being of all Americans as reducing government spending. While the distribution of the pieces of this increased economic pie is a function of the marketplace, historically everyone at every level of the income ladder benefits when an economy expands.[3]

UNCORK THE GENIE'S BOTTLE

This analysis puts in perspective the depressant effect which current levels of government spending have im-

Per Capita Share of GDP

	CURRENT SITUATION FEDERAL, STATE, AND LOCAL GOVTS. SPEND OVER 40% OF GDP		ECONOMIC GROWTH IF GOV'T. SPENDING WERE REDUCED TO 20% OF GDP	
	2% COMPOUNDED GROWTH		4% COMPOUNDED GROWTH	
	GDP	*per capita share of GDP*	GDP	*per capita share of GDP*
1987 Pop. 243 million	$4.359 trillion	$17,934	$4.359 trillion	$17,934
Over a decade (1997) Est. pop. 263 million	$5.314 trillion	$20,201	$6.45 trillion	$24,530
Over a generation (2011) Est. pop. 284 million	$7.011 trillion	$24,622	$11.174 trillion	$39,239

posed on our national economy and, hence, on each individual. Government spending is a lid on the genie's bottle—remove it and you gain the benefit of the pent-up creative juices of a dynamic society.

Liberal commentators have persisted in their claims that Reagan's tax and fiscal policies have led to "the rich getting richer and the poor, poorer." As with most generalizations, there's just enough truth in that statement for it to be dangerous. *Everyone* is getting wealthier—except for those who do not possess the knowledge or the training to participate fully in the economy. Those folks are being left behind and are poorer *relatively*—although they benefit from an improving general economy.

But all of this misses the really important point, which is that people with *already* accumulated wealth, whether very wealthy or not, have been prospering at the expense of those who are *trying* to accumulate wealth. Why? Because of unprecedented high real interest rates that benefit those who "rent" money and harm those who borrow it. Because of massive federal deficits, our national savings rate has fallen substantially. The competition for funds has risen, contributing, at least in part, to higher interest rates. Private capital investment per worker has fallen, reducing the rate of growth per hour worked.[4]

Those who are trying to accumulate wealth have been hit by higher interest rates on everything they buy—homes, cars, appliances—and on the businesses they are starting or building, and in slower wage growth because of less capital being available for investment. To create greater opportunities for those endeavoring to accumulate wealth, we need the low interest rates and low tax rates that come with reduced federal spending and deficits.

RETHINKING "COMPASSION"

Despite overwhelming evidence that increased government spending curtails economic growth, advocates of increased federal spending inevitably seek to occupy the moral high ground, claiming that fiscal conservatives have no compassion for the poor.

However, these self-anointed guardians of the public weal are not spending their money—they're spending ours. They don't write checks on their own accounts but on the Treasury's. There is nothing compassionate in taking money from Peter and redistributing it to Paul, especially if Peter is hard-working and Paul prefers collecting unemployment insurance. (I would at least grant some level of moral consistency if legislators with inherited wealth, like Ted Kennedy, turned their entire fortunes over to charity—and *then* asked you and me to "contribute" through the tax system.)

I suspect that the "compassion" of most of the liberal big spenders stems from a desire to serve the constituency that elects them— not the unorganized poor but the public employee unions and associations that organize and claim to speak for the various constituencies upon whom the bureaucrats' livelihood depends.

My compassion, on the other hand, runs to the 28-year-old divorcée who is a secretary or receptionist providing day care for her child and trying to make ends meet, but not to the unwed mother of three who has never tried to hold a job or exhibited any interest in, or capacity for, self-restraint. I don't think it is right to tax the one to support the other. And tax the one we do. Even though she may pay little or no direct personal income tax, she pays more than seven percent of her salary in social security tax and pays hidden taxes (corporate income taxes, import duties, and various fees) in everything she buys.

My compassion runs to the young family trying to buy a home and raise three children. We tax them to provide unemployment compensation to a single male who works just long enough to qualify for unemployment payments and then goes fishing until his "benefits" run out.

Tax revenues from the "rich" represent only a small portion of the support payments for those on welfare and unemployment compensation. It is working people and their entrepreneurial employers who supply the bulk of the funds. But the liberal big spenders ignore this reality in their pell-mell race to demonstrate their "compassion" for the poor.

LIBERAL HYPOCRISY

One of the reasons the liberals can get away with such hypocrisy is that the national media, by and large, shares the values of the big spenders and will not unmask them. Irving Kristol has remarked that "the popular media are pleased to sharpen and dramatize" the liberals' preoccupation with the poor because "sanctimonious compassion has always been a key element in their professional self-definition."

"But what if it can be shown that increased government spending is destructive to greater prosperity?" asks Richard W. Rahn, Chief Economist of the Chamber of Commerce of the United States. "Then, *the whole moral basis of the argument for increased government spending begins*

MYTH

For some to get richer, others have to become poorer.

REALITY

That is the mythology of the "zero-sum game." Its proponents would have you believe that our economy is like a football game—for every winner, there must be a loser. But in a dynamic, growing economy like ours, everyone wins because there's more for everyone. In a stagnant economy, everyone is penalized and there are no winners.

High taxes and excessive government spending are the sources of economic stagnation. Ironically, the liberals' justification for more taxes and spending—to aid the poor— produces the very economic stagnation and zero growth that hurts most those least able to compete.

to shrivel away. In fact, the evidence is rapidly growing that beyond a certain point (government provision of a judicial system, defense, law and order, public health, and other "public goods," including security of person and property) increases in government spending (as a percentage of GNP) become an economic hindrance; that is, *additional spending is more likely to increase economic misery than to alleviate it*"[5] (Emphasis added.)

It is clear that higher government spending reduces economic growth. Those who prefer immediate gratification through massive federal spending must answer to the poor—and to their children—why they have chosen to condemn the less fortunate to a bleak economic future.

CHAPTER 10

THE BRAWN DRAIN

Capitalism generated a new mentality, a new perception of the human condition. After the experience of capitalism anywhere people everywhere came to regard prosperity as the rule; poverty as the exception. The fact that we launched a "war on poverty" demonstrates this. No one would contemplate a war on poverty in India or Africa, where need is much more desperate than here. Only in a prosperous nation like our own, where the great war against poverty had already been won—by means of the market economy—would the elimination of the last, lingering remnants of poverty emerge as a political issue. The trouble is that if we employ the wrong remedy to eradicate the remaining pockets of poverty—as we are doing—we may find that we have destroyed prosperity instead, as in the familiar story about killing the goose that laid the golden eggs.

(Edmund A. Opitz)[1]

WHILE welfare proponents say we are relieving misery with our tax dollars, common sense tells us that we are, at least in part, *creating* it by rewarding people if they can prove that they are poor, unemployed, handicapped, or sick. Just as high marginal tax rates discourage entrepreneurial activity—leading to a "brain drain"—so, too, does the welfare state discourage people from working—leading to a "brawn drain."

After a mind-boggling trillion dollars in the "war on poverty," after quadrupling federal programs, we have more poverty than we started with.

Social scientist Charles Murray demonstrated that the federal government's efforts to combat poverty have not only failed but have actually made matters worse. The number of poor people declined until the 1960s, but as poverty spending began to rise, the number of people below the poverty line grew right along with the spending. The percentage of active workers in the labor force went down (even during economic booms) when unemployment benefits went up.[2]

Murray carefully documented changes in the law that made it profitable to get on, and stay on, welfare: AFDC (Aid to Families with Dependent Children) payments were permitted to families with able-bodied, unemployed fathers; visits to welfare homes to check eligibility were forbidden; welfare was made available to working mothers who had not previously qualified; the Supreme Court struck down the rule that a woman was not eligible for AFDC if she had a man (presumably able to work) living in the house; the Court also struck down one-year state residency requirements for welfare.[3]

Murray noted that every bit as important as a change in the welfare rules was a change in attitude about poverty. The new attitude, propagated by an academic and bureaucratic elite, was that being poor was the fault of "the system," not the fault of the individual. Social ostracism for being "on the dole" declined dramatically.[4]

"POORNESS" AS A RED BADGE
OF COURAGE

During my service as Director of the California Office of Economic Opportunity in 1970-71 for then-Governor Ronald Reagan, this transformation in attitudes became all too clear. The Federal Office of Economic Opportunity "poverty warriors" did not consider upward mobility a fact of life in a capitalist economy. They worked to organize the "poor" into a political force, urging them to "help tear down the system that had made them poor." (The "system" was, of course, the free enterprise, capitalist, market system of America.) They enshrined the poor and claimed that poverty was tangible evidence of the poor's rejection of a "corrupt system" and a proud refusal to fraternize with the "enemy." The poor were candidates for sainthood in the "new order."

Naturally, such nobility was entitled to a reward. This new conception of poverty gave birth to new terminology that, in turn, reinforced the bureaucratic structures fashioned to serve the "new poor." We moved from the "dole" to "entitlements" and from "charity cases" to "clients."

CREATION OF A POVERTY "INDUSTRY"

The federal poverty establishment, not the poor, is the biggest beneficiary of social programs. Robert Woodson, President of the National Center for Neighborhood Enterprise, has observed that "even many liberals will concede that aid has created a *poverty industry* in America. This industry accounts for hundreds of agencies and thousands of social workers, civil servants and other professionals whose business . . . rides on the backs of the poor; *about 75 percent of aid to the poor goes not to them but to those who serve the poor.*"[5] (Emphasis added.)

Economics Professor Walter Williams has calculated that if all the funds appropriated for the poor were given directly to them, a poor family of four would receive $34,000 a year. Instead, they get about $8,000. The remaining $26,000 gets gobbled up by the bureaucrats who manage the system.

The liberal big spenders in Congress know all of this as well as we do. They have the same facts available to them. They are aware of Charles Murray's work and that of others who have reached similar conclusions. Why, then, do they continue to support *federal* welfare efforts instead of getting Washington out of the welfare business, returning it to the states, local governments, private organizations, and individuals where it belongs?

THE POLITICS OF POORNESS

The answer is power and politics. The special-interest base of these politicians is the welfare bureaucracy, its satellite organizations, and the public-employee unions, all of which constitute a formidable grass-roots political force rich with campaign funds.

It is this reality that will prevent the 1988 Welfare Reform Bill from making any difference. The much-ballyhooed "workfare" provision—ostensibly to provide a *quid pro quo* ("do something in exchange for your welfare payment")—applies only to two-parent welfare families and does not start until 1994. But we've tried this

MYTH

There is a poor class in America. They will always be with us. We must accept that and take care of them.

REALITY

There will always be people who, at any given time, are poor—that is, less well off than others. Just because a person is in "tight" circumstances today does not condemn him to that condition perpetually. He may be poor in material things but rich in pride and potential.

Many of today's captains of industry were launched from modest, even poor beginnings. By the same token, people who are considered rich today may face bankruptcy tomorrow—and come out of that. We are a society in flux—mobility is the name of the game.

To refer to a class of poor suggests "once poor, always poor." But we know that's not the American experience.

Liberal welfare programs do not "cure" poverty, they perpetuate it by ensuring that some will remain poor to enjoy the benefits of poorness. A *welfare class*—not a *poor class*—has been created that will provide a "demand" for welfare so long as it is "supplied," assuring permanent employment to those who tend the poor.

and similar "reforms" before. It isn't going to work, because the federal welfare bureaucracy, threatened with loss of jobs and power, will not allow it to be successful.

The ACLU speaks for the liberal/welfare mentality in opposing work requirements as a condition of eligibility for welfare benefits.[6] ACLU's thinking is wholly alien to most Americans—but it drives the federal welfare engines in Washington. It will continue to do so as long as Washington runs welfare.

FEDERAL WELFARE A FAILURE

The only rational course is to recognize that federal welfare has failed utterly. This country managed to get along for a century-and-a-half without national welfare and always found ways to help those down on their luck. It is only in the last few decades that we have turned to Washington and received a massive welfare headache for our trouble.

A case in point is what the emergence of Washington-dominated welfare has done to the so-called "settlement houses," of which there are some 600 across the nation. These houses are located in the midst of the neighborhoods they serve and offer a variety of services tailored to local needs. They were started and funded by private benefactors. *The Wall Street Journal* reported on the Henry Street Settlement House in New York City, which is nearly 100 years old:

> Settlement workers . . . are the infantry in the battle against social decay, and it is their intimate, day-to-day involvement with the needy that sets settlement houses apart from much of the welfare establishment.

Henry Street offers a supermarket of social services under one roof—and in the neighborhood where its clients live. (The name settlement derives from the practice of early reformers to "settle" among the poor they served.)

The center's approach contrasts sharply with the government's, where a maze of agencies offer ever more specialized "boutique" services to the poor, who often flounder under the complexity and indifference of the system.

By tradition, settlement houses addressed the root causes of social problems, rather than merely provided Band-Aid relief. Today, that philosophy is being challenged—some say compromised—by their increasing reliance on public financing.[7]

Henry Street operated on a privately-funded budget of $800,000 in 1965, just as the "war on poverty" was being launched. By 1986, its budget was $7.4 million (a 900 percent increase), of which nearly 80 percent came from government sources. Just as with many of the poor themselves, we have lured their (previously) privately funded benefactors into the federal welfare web. Now largely dependent on Washington, these agencies must dance to the federal welfare tune to keep the funds flowing, emphasizing the particular programs that are in vogue in Washington.

Settlements have adapted to survive. When government funds for job-training and youth programs were cut, San Diego's Neighborhood House dropped them and concentrated on the Head Start and mental-health programs still in favor. Anthony Wagner, the head of the Pillsbury United settlement in Minneapolis, complains that good grant-seekers aren't necessarily the best street workers. "What the funders want are people who are articulate, who can

write well. What I need are people who can go into a group
of black teenagers and say, 'Get yourselves together, you
—,' and be respected for saying it."[8]

WELFARE "ENTREPRENEURSHIP" AT THE LOCAL LEVEL

Several years ago, Sacramento County, California, tried a
settlement house approach for welfare recipients. The supervisors established a dormitory center called "Bannon
Street" with 200 beds, food service, and other facilities.
Cash grants, which had been the norm, were discontinued
in favor of the full-service center. Although more than 200
people had been receiving cash grants, the 200 beds were
never filled. This experience confirmed that many of the
cash-grant recipients had other means of support. It allowed the supervisors to distinguish between the truly
needy and those that were not.

Residents of Bannon Street had to help maintain it, they
had to train for a job, and they had to make a serious effort
to look for work. A *quid pro quo* was demanded and
received, and as a result, a sense of pride emerged among
the residents. The center provided a "home and family"
for many who had no friends or relatives in the area. A
sense of community and mutual support developed.

Everything was progressing well until Legal Services
of Northern California, a federally funded poverty lawyer
program, filed a lawsuit seeking to close Bannon Street on
grounds that it violated the poor's right to privacy by
forcing them to come to a central facility. Unfortunately,
California's Supreme Court—led by Rose Bird—decided
against Sacramento County, and the facility was closed.
Later it was revealed that the "client" for whom the Legal

Services attorneys filed the action had not wanted the facility closed. He had found it to be a fine support system for himself and others. The training and job placement provided by Bannon Street had been more effective than any other such efforts of the County.

Sacramento County responded to the Supreme Court decision by increasing its cash grants and eliminating the residence requirement. The predictable happened. Every "king of the road" for hundreds of miles around found it advantageous to travel to Sacramento once a month to get his general assistance cash grant of $257. "We hear story after story of people coming from out of state who learned about our aid program through a hobo camp," Deputy Social Services Director Penelope Clark said. "A person from Oregon won't come all the way down here to Sacramento to spend a night or two in Bannon Street. But for a $257 check, they'll come."[9]

In a single year following the Court decision and the return to cash grants, the number of general assistance grant recipients rose from 4,000 to 5,000, and costs rose from just over $6 million to more than $9 million. Local welfare officials, concerned that much of the money simply perpetuated a lifestyle of drugs and alcoholism, proposed reopening of Bannon Street, offering shelter and food in-kind to transients, rather than cash.[10] Legal Services responded predictably: "A mandatory aid-in-kind program would have a dramatic negative effect on our most *victimized citizens.*"[11] (Emphasis added.)

TAKE WHAT IS OFFERED OR GO WITHOUT

The Sacramento County Board of Supervisors approved a restoration of the in-kind approach for transient general assistance applicants. Essentially, the Board has said that *it*, not the recipients, would dictate the terms of the handouts.[12] The elected officials will set the rules of the game—a refreshing change for the taxpayer.

The Board's decision to reopen Bannon Street might have been influenced, at least in part, by the fact that the makeup of California's Supreme Court has changed dramatically since the Bannon Street decision. In 1986, Rose Bird and other liberals on the Court were rejected by substantial margins at the polls by California voters. The Court is now controlled by a conservative majority. Malcolm Lucas, the new Chief Justice, wrote the dissenting opinion in the Bannon Street case, stating that in-kind aid "does not reflect any inhumanity. The same choice exists for other general assistance recipients: take what is offered or go without."[13]

•

We should be grateful that high deficits and tightened budgets are forcing us to review the functions of the federal government, including its management of the welfare system. Wholly independent of financial considerations (which are serious enough by themselves), we should recognize that Washington cannot and should not be the welfare czar.

The management circuits of the federal government are seriously overloaded, and we must pare back its functions in order to enable it to discharge effectively those things that only the federal government can do. Welfare is properly the subject of state, local, and private action.

CHAPTER 11

YOUR TAXES USED AGAINST YOU

> That to compel a man to furnish contributions of money for the propagation of opinions which he disbelieves is sinful and tyrannical.
> (Virginia Statute of Religious Freedom, *1786*)[1]

IN the dark of night, bundles of cash are loaded onto armored trucks from the Treasury of the United States and taken to waiting planes at Andrews Air Force Base just outside Washington. Billions of dollars in all denominations are loaded aboard the planes. The aircraft taxi into position and head east in formation. Well over the Atlantic Ocean they drop down to a thousand feet, the cargo doors open, and billions are dumped into the sea.

An incredible waste? You will be stunned to learn that you would be far better off if many of the dollars that you send to Washington were dumped in the Atlantic rather than spent—because they are spent to oppose and undermine the values and way of life that you hold dear. That is the reality of our current situation.

The taxpayer should not be coerced (taxed) to support lifestyles, values, and activities with which he does not agree. *How* taxes are used probably causes as much dissension among taxpayers as *how much* taxpayers are required to pay.

Under the best of circumstances there will be someone

who objects to certain uses of his tax dollars—such as the pacifist who objects to supporting national defense. *But one of the basic tenets of responsive, effective government is to engage in only those activities for which there is broad citizen consensus and support.*

WAR ON POVERTY

Lyndon Johnson's war on poverty launched a new era in the federal government's relationship with its citizens. Tax dollars were funnelled to individuals and organizations whose announced purposes were to disrupt American society, to bite the hand that feeds. The Office of Economic Opportunity was populated with grantmakers who handed out funds to the most radical, outrageous "poverty" programs. Anyone who proposed challenging "the establishment" was likely to get funded.

Since the launching of the War on Poverty a quarter-century ago, many agencies and programs have become part of the "assault team," directly challenging societal norms. We have seen God and Christmas driven out of our classrooms, and birth control and abortion counseling (without parental notification) injected into our schools. Your tax money has poured into private organizations that promote feminist causes and "alternative" lifestyles. Grants to "artists" have been made for trashy poetry and outlandish visual art projects.

Billions of tax dollars have been allocated to the "war" on AIDS. Of those, millions are spent on AIDS "education"—with substantial grants to gay and lesbian organizations. Their materials condone and encourage homosexuality.

Gay Men's Health Crisis, Inc., of New York, which

received more than $600,000 from the federal government, distributed an AIDS "comic" book depicting in explicit detail an encounter between two homosexual men.

The materials included a "Social Skills Development" program that involved "asking someone for his phone number, meeting someone new at a bar and letting him know you are interested in having sex, and negotiating a contract for safe sex, discussing your sexual limits"; writing a personal sexual advertisement for *The New York Native,* a "gay" magazine; "Guidelines for Healthy Sex," to promote "satisfying, erotic alternatives to high risk sexual practices; identifying erogenous areas of the body other than the genitals that produce an erotic response . . . use of safe sex photos as a sexual enrichment tool."[2]

That's how some of *your* tax dollars are spent by *your* government in Washington.

•

"LEGAL SERVICES"—
THE POVERTY LAWYERS

No single instrument of the federal government has been more central to the assault on the values of the average American taxpayer than federal legal services—the so-called "poverty lawyers."

Legal Services was part of the Office of Economic Opportunity from its inception in the 1960s until the early 1970s when the "poverty law" functions were transferred to a quasi-independent agency—the Legal Services Corporation (LSC). LSC, whose board is appointed by the President with the advice and consent of the Senate, receives all its funding from the federal government—more than $300 million annually.

Traditional lawyers volunteered to solve the domestic relations, landlord-tenant, and bankruptcy problems of poor people who could not afford lawyers' fees. But as Clark Durant, the Reagan-appointed Chairman of Legal Services Corporation, has observed, the federal poverty lawyers had a very different agenda. They launched a *movement* "to eradicate poverty and bring about social reform." "The Legal Services *movement*," Durant suggests, "involved a shift from a concept of *demand* to a concept of *need*. To determine the number and needs of eligible clients, we rely not on individually articulated demands . . . the poor, according to this rationale, are unable to know what they should be asking for. Needs and priorities are established by community surveys and local leaders, not by individual clients."[3]

POVERTY LAWYERS ATTACK TAXPAYERS' VALUES

In their comprehensive study, "Destroying Democracy— How Government Funds Partisan Politics," James T. Bennett and Thomas J. DiLorenzo detailed the LSC's pivotal role in the use of taxpayer funds to oppose taxpayers and their values.[4]

They noted that in 1979-81, Legal Services lawyers in Montana, Iowa, and Connecticut sued to force the use of state tax funds for sex-change operations; that California Rural Legal Assistance sued the University of California to block research that would improve the efficiency of farm machinery because it might displace farm workers;

and that a Legal Services lawyer in Texas filed a lawsuit to establish free public education as a constitutional right for illegal aliens.[5]

Bennett and DiLorenzo's investigation also revealed that the Bay Area (Tampa, Florida) Legal Services sued to prevent statewide literacy tests as a prerequisite for high school graduation; and that poverty lawyers in Maine, Massachusetts, Colorado, and South Carolina sued on behalf of various Indian tribes to lay claim to hundreds of thousands of acres (two-thirds of the state of Maine should be turned over to the Pasamaquoddy and Penobscot Indians, LSC lawyers claimed).[6]

Economist and syndicated columnist Walter Williams revealed a U.S. Inspector General finding that LSC lawyers violated the law when they campaigned against a California ballot initiative that sought to reduce the state income tax.

Williams, commenting on the poverty lawyers' assault on the family, noted that the LSC had assisted the Committee to Defend Reproductive Rights, seeking to block a California initiative by which citizens sought to halt state-funded abortions, and the same lawyers argued (before the U.S. Supreme Court) that teenage girls have a constitutional right to abortion *without* knowledge or consent of their parents.[7]

In her monograph, "Legal Services Corporation vs. The Family," Kathleen deBettencourt points out that, over the last quarter century, Legal Services attorneys have either initiated or joined in lawsuits with the following objectives:

- to provide welfare payments to a young mother living with a man irrespective of whether they were married;

- to provide welfare payments for illegitimate as well as legitimate children;

- to ignore the income of other members of the family unit when determining eligibility for welfare;

- to ignore the income of parents of an unwed mother living at home when determining her eligibility for welfare;

- to provide welfare benefits to minor children who insist on living apart from their families;

- to broaden availability of food stamps from families to unrelated people living together;

- to prevent parental notification and the need for parental approval when a minor daughter seeks an abortion;

- to prevent parents from committing their minor children to mental institutions;

- to establish that a homosexual parent has an equal right to custody of a minor child as a heterosexual parent.[8]

And this is only a partial, representative list. deBettencourt concludes: "The history of the Legal Services Corporation and its grantees strongly suggests that the actions of grantees, far from strengthening the family, have undermined the very root assumptions undergirding a culture based on the family. Family law, once the province of the states, has increasingly been superseded by a national family policy promulgated, not by Congress, but by federal courts and grantees of the Legal Services Corporation."[9]

PLAYING POLITICS WITH TAX DOLLARS

Bennett and DiLorenzo also found blatant political activity on the part of the LSC:

> LSC has been clearly riddled with illegal political activity. Hundreds of millions of taxpayers' dollars have been used to fund the political goals of a determined group that has used the needs of the poor as an excuse to obtain vast sums of money from the government. Tax monies have been diverted to elect candidates to office, to defeat or support legislation at all levels of government, to finance administrative and congressional lobbying, to organize at the grass-roots level for political purposes, and to fund a host of allied organizations.[10]

The extent of the poverty lawyer's involvement in politics is no more obvious than in redistricting—the process of designing new congressional districts—following the 1980 census. On their own initiative—without a request from any poor client—various LSC organizations in New Mexico, Texas, California, and elsewhere involved themselves in redistricting. In part this was to help create a Congress filled with members who would support LSC against the Reagan Administration that was intent on curtailing or eliminating LSC. This was part of LSC's "survival plan" that was launched following Reagan's victory in 1980.

In 1984, the Reagan-appointed Board of Legal Services conducted an investigation of the redistricting activities of various Legal Services offices. Many of the local offices refused to cooperate or provide any information regarding the use of taxpayer funds on redistricting lawsuits. Like a mutinous crew, the poverty lawyers defied their commanders. The investigation revealed that over 28,000 hours and $600,000 had been spent on such cases. That appeared to be only a fraction of the time and money devoted to such political action.[11]

TAXPAYERS HELPED DEFEAT BORK NOMINATION

The poverty lawyers became part of the nationwide network of liberals in opposition to the nomination of Robert Bork to the United States Supreme Court. On September 2, 1987, the National Legal Aid and Defenders Association (NLADA), supported in a substantial way by LSC grants and dues, distributed to LSC groups around the nation a political action packet. It contained a range of materials with which to attack Bork. Of course the cover letter urged the recipient to act only on his own time—the refuge of those who know they are engaged in prohibited activities.

In the cover letter, Clint Lyons, Executive Director of NLADA and former Vice President of LSC under Carter, said, "This is a fight of unprecedented proportions and every single contact is important." The flier included sample letters to senators, their addresses and phone numbers, sample editorials prepared by People for the American Way, and a "Fact Sheet on Robert Bork" by Alliance for Justice, an affiliate of NOW, National Abortion Rights League, and Americans for Democratic Action, among others.

LEGAL SERVICES RADICAL AGENDA

More recently, in July 1988, Texas Rural Legal Aid, Inc., came to the aid of Veterans Peace Convoy. As about 15 trucks loaded with supplies for the Nicaraguan (Marxist) Sandinistas tried to cross the border into Mexico, some were stopped by U.S. Border Patrol and Customs agents. The Texas poverty lawyers joined in a suit against Secretary of States George Schultz to allow the vehicles to go to Nicaragua. How this helps with the legal needs of poor Americans was not disclosed.

The radical nature of LSC becomes most apparent in its attitude toward American business:

> The *"social agenda"* pursued by the LSC is largely an anti-business agenda. Legal Services activists are part of a political movement that views the American free enterprise system as a giant conspiracy, whereby a small group of oppressors" dominate "the people." According to a book published by the LSC, people "feel *the oppression* of power companies, transit companies, clinics, landlords and the like most strongly," although the worst oppressors are "the bankers, insurance companies, corporate directors, etc., which for all practical purposes hold ultimate influence."[12] (Emphasis added.)

Listen to those words and phrases—and hear the statement of an instructor at an LSC-funded political training conference: "[C]apitalism is . . . a . . . power which bankrupts cities, which destroys jobs, which creates poverty and economic chaos. . . . Now that the corporate program is creating ruin in the economy . . . *the most important thing we can do in the coming years is to keep up the anti-corporate campaign.*"[13] (Emphasis added.)

And the Washington representative of an LSC-supported Association of Community Organizations for Reform Now (ACORN) declared: "*I am a socialist.* It's because society is based on collectivity and interpersonal relationships that capitalism will fail."[14] (Emphasis added.)

POVERTY LAWYERS COZY WITH CONGRESS

Why on earth do we continue to provide federal funds for the LSC and for its "National Support Centers" which have been described as "think tanks for the radical left?"[15] The Reagan administration tried to eliminate LSC funding in each of its budgets. But the LSC, with offices in virtually every state and congressional district, has become a formidable lobbying force. It has formed political alliances with the liberal big spenders on Capitol Hill:

> Those in Congress who support LSC appropriations and do not question how the funds are spent are supported at election time by the grass roots organizations nurtured by LSC. Thus, a cozy relationship has developed between those in Congress who appropriate funds and those who spend them. The taxpayers are the losers, for they finance the grass roots political activity that sends to Congress those individuals who benefit from the illegal use of tax money and who have every incentive to continue this practice.[16]

Why then not place firm statutory limits on its political, lobbying, and social agenda (class action) activities? That has been tried time and time again. But the LSC radicals have ignored these restrictions.

When Ronald Reagan was elected in 1980, LSC lawyers felt threatened—and justifiably so. They knew Reagan would appoint a Board of Directors for LSC that would come down hard on various LSC offices around the nation. The poverty lawyers wanted to remain free of any restraints on their activities. They developed a "survival plan" designed to insulate themselves from presidential control or discipline.

On their way out the door in 1981, Clint Lyons and Senior Grant Administrator Buckey Askew funnelled about $19 million from LSC to NLADA to finance their "survival plan." Both Lyons and Askew followed their grant dollars and were given high positions at NLADA (Clint Lyon as Executive Director).

"AUTOMATIC PILOT" FUNDING FOR L.S.C.

With the help of their friends in Congress, the LSC lawyers became virtually autonomous, assured of perpetual funding irrespective of need or performance, free to continue their activist and political shenanigans.

Through appropriations riders, Congress has prohibited the (Reagan-appointed) LSC [Board] from spending money to enforce many of the restrictions Congress earlier imposed. And Congress has crippled [the] LSC's [Board's] ability to investigate such abuses by placing restrictions on reporting and monitoring of LSC grantees. *These grantees [the various poverty lawyer offices around the nation] are exempt from the reporting requirements that apply to vir-*

*tually all other recipients of federal funds. They also need
not compete for grants. There is even an explicit "grand-
father" provision that guarantees funding for past recipients, no matter how inefficient or ineffective they may be.*
Theoretically, [the] LSC [Board] still has authority to defund grantees that explicitly violate the law, but the process
is so cumbersome that it takes months and costs hundreds
of thousands of dollars to defund even the most flagrant
violators."[17] (Emphasis added.)

Congress cut the LSC poverty lawyer offices loose from
the control and management of the Board of Directors of
LSC. We have to fund them, but they can operate as they
please. The inmates have really seized control of the asylum. Bennett and DiLorenzo concluded:

[The LSC poverty lawyers] do not see the civil legal problems of the poor as their principal concern; rather, their
emphasis is on achieving social and political change
through the judicial process and on redistributing income
and wealth by expanding the welfare system through use of
the courts. . . . Under these organizations' ruse of providing access for the poor to the justice system, *the taxpayers
are being forced to finance social and economic policy
changes that many of them would oppose."*[18] (Emphasis
added.)

Truly, American taxpayers would be better off today if
funds appropriated for the poverty lawyers had instead
been "buried at sea." The direct costs of the LSC have
been high enough. The indirect costs, on the other hand,
are incalculable, because they involve increased expenditures by a multitude of federal, state, and local agencies,
court congestion, friction between parent and child, cre-

ation of "rights" without responsibilities, assaults on business, and general political combat.

How many times have you heard the big-spending liberals on Capitol Hill lament that "we have cut the budget to the bone. All the fat is gone. Only muscle is left." The Legal Services Corporation is not "fat," or even government waste, as we normally speak of it. Legal Services is *muscle*—the muscle of the radical left. It's about time we excised that muscle.

•

When government spends money on social programs—education, poverty lawyers, welfare, etc.—as distinguished from defense, roads, parks, etc.—government is in the "values" game. Taxpayer supported social programs necessarily inculcate one set of values or another. Even a concerted effort on the part of a teacher, for example, to be values-neutral communicates to children the notion that values are unimportant or, at most, relative and situational. Since there is no such thing as a values-neutral environment or a values-free education, the question is, who is going to decide what values are propagated? The one who pays the piper, of course, for he decides the tune.

The more of his earnings that are taken in taxes and spent by others whose values may be alien to his, the less power the citizen has to shape a society to his liking. Taxes are much more than a financial burden to the citizen taxpayer. In the hands of government his tax dollars are at best stripped of their power to promulgate his values; at worst his tax dollars are weapons that can be used against him.

CHAPTER 12

UNMASKING THE "DEMAND" FOR SERVICES

> If we can prevent the government from wasting the labors of the people, under the pretense of taking care of them, they must become happy.
>
> *(Thomas Jefferson)*[1]

POLITICIANS frequently claim that a "demand" exists for more and bigger programs and spending. But this "demand" is not demand as we ordinarily understand it—in the context of supply and demand. Why? Because most government services cost the recipient very little, if anything. There is no price to regulate demand—hence "demand" is virtually unlimited.

If one of your local auto dealers decided to "market" cars *free*, the "demand" would be virtually limitless. If you visited your favorite shoe store and found that $50 shoes were on sale for 50 cents a pair, your "demand" for shoes would probably be limited only by your closet space.

In 1972, to help develop Proposition 1 (the constitutional tax and spending limit for California) for then-Governor Ronald Reagan, we commissioned a study to learn how much citizens knew about taxes and government spending. One section was devoted to the costs of various government services. Under the direction of Wm. Craig Stubblebine, Professor of Economics at Claremont McKenna College, our experts calculated the cost to each citizen of various state and local services—roads, education, police, prisons, garbage collection, etc.—based upon income levels. With this information in hand, we found that those surveyed underestimated the cost to them of government services by 50 to 70 percent, irrespective of income level![2] In other words, if the real cost to that person for a particular service was $100, he estimated the cost to be in a range of $30 to $50. Respondents had no idea of the real costs because of a lack of pricing information. There is no reason to believe we would get different answers today or that guesses about federally supplied services would be any more accurate.

"FREE MONEY," UNLIMITED DEMAND

And remember, the respondents to our survey were taxpayers who were actually paying something for the services. When you have a person who is paying no taxes and is receiving a welfare grant, food stamps, medicare, etc., there is absolutely no limitation on that person's demand for more (or on the orchestration of a political cacophony by welfare worker unions and others who "tend" the poor). In the case of "welfare" to businesses and the nonpoor—farm subsidies, transportation grants, medical research support, etc.—some of the recipients do pay taxes, but because there is no linkage between taxes paid by that individual/organization and the federal grant, Washington's funding is considered "free" money. Hence, there is little or no suppression of demand in this instance, either.

The National Council on Public Works Improvement, created at the time "infrastructure" was the buzzword around Washington, has demonstrated clearly what pricing can do with respect to the demand for capital improvements. In its report, the Council experienced:

> an average 50 percent reduction in the size of major deep draft ports on the national wish list as soon as the port cities were assigned larger shares of the cost. One such project was in Baltimore, where local interests supported a $300 million double-width channel 55 feet deep, provided it was at full *federal* expense. After beneficiaries were required to pay half the cost, the locals supported a one-way channel at a shallower depth, costing $50 million.

> Council researchers also reported that changing the federal match for sewer treatment plants from 75 percent federal money to 55 percent federal money resulted in new plants that were 30 percent less expensive.[3]

When you put a pricetag on what had been a "free lunch," it's amazing how quickly the dieting instinct surfaces.

The very fact that price is largely unavailable to ration government services is one of the most compelling reasons that less, not more, should be done by government— especially by the federal government. The more resources that are pumped into a system that has no pricing mechanism by which to ration those resources, the greater the waste, inefficiency, and popular discontent that are experienced. Pricing, and price competition, are the only things that produce reliable levels of demand—and the supply to meet it. (Privatizing the delivery of public services and converting to user fees have been successful means of reducing inefficiency and waste in such services as garbage collection, operation of penal systems, highways, etc.)

OPPORTUNITY COSTS

Another side of the "demand-for-government-services" issue is what the economists like to call "opportunity costs." This means simply that to do one thing, you have to give up the opportunity to do another. For instance, if the government taxes an Ohio businessman to pay an Iowa farmer *not* to grow corn—after routing the money through the bureaucrats in Washington—the Ohio businessman has that much less money to finance added production space, new equipment, and create more jobs—and we have nothing to show for it because we paid the farmer to do nothing. That's a very high opportunity cost.

Let's not forget, only those businesses that produce a profit are taxed. They are the winners in effective use of *their* resources. The losers don't pay taxes. They go bankrupt or run to the federal government for a subsidy or handout. If we bet on the winners to keep on winning in terms of economic growth and job creation—by letting them reinvest more of their earnings rather than taxing them away—we'd all be better off.

We must not allow our legislators to succumb to the "demands" for more government services from people who neither know nor care what the price of those services really is.

CHAPTER 13

"ASK NOT . . ."

Were we directed from Washington when to sow and when to reap, we should soon want bread.

(Thomas Jefferson)[1]

THAT spending is out of control in Washington is hardly surprising. The government is trying to do far more than it is able to handle. The pro-spending forces have grown so virulent that they inhibit the restraint mechanisms (what few are left) just as a deadly virus overwhelms the natural defense mechanisms of the human body.

The cries of anguish over reduced federal spending (in most instances merely limitations on the *rate of growth*, not actual reductions from the prior year's spending) are not prompted by concern for the nation's welfare but are the lamentations of people who are on the receiving end of one redistribution program or another.

The evidence that has been accumulating, just a small portion of which we've had an opportunity to discuss, demonstrates clearly that the American people would be much better served by reducing the size, scope and cost of the federal government. *We should view the need to make major changes in federal spending as a chance to streamline and improve the functioning of our government, not as a calamity.*

A generation ago, John F. Kennedy laid down a challenge to America: "Ask not what your country can do for

you but what you can do for your country." Lyndon Johnson soon responded with the War on Poverty. It communi-
cated the following messages—to some it said, "You
don't have to ask; we'll give it to you," and to others it
said, "You don't have to do anything for your country—
except send money." The War on Poverty proved once
again that government cannot solve problems by throwing
money at them. Government creates problems which it
then impoverishes the Nation trying to solve.

*It's time for a new theme befitting our bicentennial: "Ask
not what your country can do for you—period!"*

RETURN LOCAL PROBLEMS TO
LOCAL PROBLEM SOLVERS

For most people, getting the federal government off their
backs and out of their pockets is all they ask. For those
who do need some assistance, it is an essentially local
problem. Washington must give local problems back to
local problem solvers. Far from creating a hardship, such a
realignment of responsibilities will produce better results
because each locale is unique and can generate solutions
befitting that uniqueness.

More than a decade ago, about the time of the first oil
"crisis," we were bombarded with the notion that we had
entered an "era of limits." Whether or not that concept
had validity with respect to natural resources, it is absolutely on target with respect to the federal government
today. We have reached and exceeded our limits in terms
of financial resources, witness the continuing huge deficits. We are at the limit—and beyond—of Congress' and

the President's capacity to manage a government of the size and complexity of the federal structure today.

WASHINGTON "CONGLOMERATE" UNMANAGEABLE

The federal government is like a vast corporate "conglomerate" which is choking to death on its "acquisitions." The recent spate of corporate takeovers and leveraged buyouts are premised on the notion that large conglomerates are not capable of managing their diverse enterprises effectively. When the parts are sold to others who can manage them properly, those parts individually have greater total value than the parent company. What remains after the sell-off is a core business that is of manageable size and scope. Any competent board of directors would insist that Washington "spin off" a vast array of its functions to state and local governments, privatize much of what is left and wind up with a federal structure that is lean, mean and manageable.

Congress creates new programs and agencies, pushes them out the door and rarely revisits them. Oversight— Congress's responsibility to track the activities of government—is hard work and earns few political points. Except for high visibility hearings that enable them to bring discredit on their political enemies, congressmen do little of this kind of scut work. For all practical purposes, the federal government is entirely too large for Congress to oversee in any meaningful way.

Increasingly, presidents have gotten themselves into hot water over some blunder that can be explained, at least in part, by an impossible workload. The President is ceremonial chief of state, manager of the government, leader of his political party, moral leader of the country, media star, world traveler and is also supposed to know about a federal grant for improving the sewers in Peoria. If we want him to be effective in carrying out the functions which can be performed only by the federal government—national defense, foreign affairs, international security, international trade and monetary policy, etc.—we simply must relieve him of many domestic burdens.

G.R.H. HAS HELPED—SOME

Through the efforts of Ronald Reagan and some members of Congress, there has been a modest check on the growth of the federal government for the first time in decades. The 1985 Gramm-Rudman-Hollings Emergency Deficit Reduction Act (GRH) provided a framework for reducing spending and deficits. Undoubtedly GRH has kept deficits smaller than they might otherwise have been. But, as Chart 1 makes altogether too obvious, the GRH targets have been honored in the breach by a Congress unable and unwilling to discipline itself. When the GRH "shoe" pinches, Congress changes the deficit targets—and then still misses them.

Only a tax limitation/balanced budget amendment will make permanent what GRH has tried to achieve on an emergency basis. As Senator Phil Gramm is fond of saying, "GRH is the engagement. The tax limitation/balanced budget amendment is the marriage—it makes budget discipline *permanent.*"

A "spending freeze" is a first cousin to GRH. If

Congress and the Gramm-Rudman-Hollings (GRH) Deficit Targets

Fiscal Years	1986	1987	1988	1989	1990
GRH projections (1985)	172	144	108	72	36
Reagan budget projections (Feb. 1986)	203	144	94	68	36
GRH projections as revised in 1987	—	—	144	136	100
Reagan budget projections (Feb. 1988)	—	—	147	130	104
Actual deficits	221	150	155	162*	?

* *Estimate: Budget of the United States Government, FY–1990.*

adopted—*and honored*—it can achieve a balanced budget by 1993, for as Chart 1 reveals, revenues of the federal government have increased an average of nine percent per year since 1983, while federal spending has increased about six percent. We don't need a tax increase. Ever-greater tax revenues will simply accommodate and encourage more spending.

A spending freeze is a stopgap measure. It does not require the termination of federal programs. But sooner or later we must terminate programs and streamline the federal structure so as to achieve and maintain a balanced budget. (To provide a framework for setting priorities, and to demonstrate how the FY-1989 budget might have been in balance, we have included Postscript 1 to this chapter.)

CONGRESS MAKES MATTERS WORSE

The federal government is "broke"—both figuratively and literally. We have a total systems failure, a "brown

Chart 1

Growth of Federal Spending

		RECEIPTS			OUTLAYS			DEFICIT
Year	Total	Yearly $ Increase	Yearly % Increase	Total	Yearly $ Increase	Yearly % Increase		
1983	$601[1]	—	—	$ 808	—	—		−$208
84	667	66	11	852	44	5		− 185
Actual[2]								
85	734	67	10	946	94	11		− 212
86	769	35	5	990	44	5		− 221
87	854	85	11	1,005	15	1.5		− 150
Estimated[3]								
1988	908	54	6	1,062	57	6		− 154
89	988	80	9	1,134	72	7		− 146
Amount by which Receipt/Outlay Base has Increased from 1983–89	$387 (64%)			$ 326 (40%)				
Average Annual Increase in Receipts/ Outlays from 1983–89		$65	9%		$54	5%		

[1] $ Figures and percentages have been rounded.

[2] Budget of the United States.

[3] US Chamber of Commerce, Forecasting Section: "Economic Outlook," September/October 1988, p. 2.

MYTH

The Gramm-Rudman-Hollings Emergency Deficit Reduction Act of 1985 (GRH), or something similar, will solve our deficit problem. We don't need a constitutional amendment to get our fiscal house in order.

REALITY

GRH is only a statute. As such, it can be ignored or even repealed by Congress. Its deficit targets have been changed frequently by a Congress unwilling to live up to its own commitments.

GRH has helped to slow the rate of increase in federal spending, but it offers nothing by way of permanent control over excessive federal spending. As Sen. Phil Gramm himself has said: GRH is the engagement; the tax limitation/balanced budget amendment is the marriage—it makes budget discipline permanent.

Only a constitutional amendment can control the operation of our government. A mere statute simply cannot get the job done. Laws control men; only the Constitution can control government.

out." Instead of stepping back to see how order might be restored, Congress has made matters worse. In both 1986 and 1987, Congress virtually subverted the constitutionally-mandated fiscal check and balance: the presidential veto power. It sent the President $600 billion omnibus spending bills, essentially daring him to veto them and shut the entire government down. This is merely the latest in a long list of congressional strategies designed to prevent the President from coming down hard on excessive spending. Congress has limited the President's ability to impound funds and defer expenditures and has denied the President even a limited, statutory test of the line-item veto.

Given that the federal structure *will not* discipline itself and that non-constitutional reforms *are not equal* to the task, the people must act through the only means available—the Constitution. Congress must abide by the Constitution. So, too, must the President and the entire federal establishment.

THE PEOPLE WANT A BALANCED BUDGET AMENDMENT

A balanced budget amendment to the United States Constitution consistently receives the support of more than three-fourths of the American people. Intuitively, the people know that corralling Congress and the federal establishment can be accomplished only through the Constitution.

Critics claim that Congress is merely a reflection of the American people. People want spending, they say. Therefore, a constitutional amendment requiring a balanced budget and limiting spending will go the way of the prohibition amendment. This is a phony analogy. The special interests of that time—the women's temperance

MYTH

If we must cut federal spending, it is only fair that both defense and social spending should bear the cuts equally.

REALITY

This is one of the most dangerous and misleading myths of all. Faced with the need to reduce our spending, we must review priorities. The first question is what functions can be performed only by the federal government and what functions can be performed by others.

Logic and our Constitution make it clear that defense and foreign affairs are uniquely the province of the national government. Whatever we must spend to do these adequately must have first call on the Treasury. If we do not successfully defend America and our nation falls prey to totalitarian adversaries, our so-called "social programs" will vanish overnight. The single most important social program in America today is defense.

Reasonable men and women may disagree as to the level of funding necessary for a proper defense. But it should be axiomatic that defense take priority over all other spending.

movement—produced prohibition; Americans didn't like that "limit" and "voted" against it by frequenting speakeasies and buying bootleg whiskey.

Today, the people *want a limit* on Washington. It is precisely because *the people* want a constitutional limit in the form of a tax limitation/balanced budget amendment that such an amendment can be honored. Spending pressures will remain, but a constitutional rule will control those inclined toward excessive spending and provide a predictable fiscal outcome.

The fiscal result we observe in Washington now is perfectly consistent with the operative incentives. If we want a different, but equally predictable, outcome, we must have a new rule with transcendant power. Only a constitutional fiscal rule possesses that power.

LIMIT INCUMBENCY

In the same vein, by adopting new rules we can change the character of Congress, diffuse the concentration of career-minded liberal big spenders and attract capable fiscal conservatives who will aid in the enforcement of a tax limitation/balanced budget amendment. The Founders considered service in the Congress as a public trust to be exercised with great restraint. They did not intend the concentration of power in Washington which has become the hallmark of our era. They never dreamed of a career-oriented, self-perpetuating elite.

The 1989 congressional pay-raise controversy unmasked the arrogance, self-indulgence, and cynicism of Congress as an institution for many Americans who had previously taken little interest in or even known much about *their* Congress. But they know now. And having forced Congress to back down, the American people have tasted blood. Now they talk openly of the possibility of congressional reforms that would have seemed fantasies only months before.

February 8, 1989, the day Congress was forced by the American people to reject its coveted pay raise, could well mark a turning point in America's relationship with its Congress. What a fitting bicentennial toast to our Founders if we seize this opportunity to invoke fundamental (constitutional) congressional reform.

What should we seek to achieve? A Congress composed of citizens who are *service*, not *career* oriented; who are *of* the people, not *above* them; who retain a *fiduciary*, instead of a *proprietary* attitude with respect to Congress's programs and activities; who must live under the laws they pass; who are gainfully employed in a real business, profession or job "back home" throughout their service in the Congress; who are respectful of the role and prerogatives of the states, local governments, and the people in their private capacities. There are many in Congress today who exhibit some or all of these characteristics—but they are a minority. They will never achieve a majority unless we reform the Congress itself. In Postscript 2 to this chapter, I have set forth the elements of a Congressional Reform Amendment that would produce these results—and more.

THE CONSTITUTION IS <u>OUR</u> ONLY WEAPON

There is another reason for us to resort to the Constitution to restore fiscal order—because it is the *only* weapon available to *us*. The liberals have created a whole range of "life support" systems for their ideology, despite its consistent rejection by the voters at presidential elections.

Liberals have created departments, agencies, and programs that live on long after the power to create them has waned. Like an army in battle, the liberals have constructed fortifications along the way to defend the ground they have gained. Past liberal successes have become "institutionalized" in many powerful ways:

- Through a judiciary whose activist opinions have amounted to "legislation" creating a body of law which could never have mustered a majority in Congress;

- Through radically gerrymandered congressional districts which give big spenders 60 percent of the House seats at the same time that they garner only 50 percent of the votes cast in House races;

- Through a Washington establishment the very size and power of which is a product of liberal big spending;

- Through a vast bureaucracy which has so much political momentum that it is on virtual "automatic pilot" funding;

- Through a national media overwhelmingly sympathetic to liberalism.

Our institution, *our* bulwark against big-spending liberalism, is the one created for us by the Founders—our Constitution. It is the medium through which government power and size can be limited. The Founders thought they had done a pretty good job of limiting the federal government—but we have allowed those limits to erode. Fortunately, the Founders were not possessed of a sense of their own infallibility. They provided for ways to amend the Constitution as the need to do so was revealed.

CHICKEN AND EGG—CONSTITUTION AND CHARACTER

Some of our philosophical brethren do not share our enthusiasm for constitutional reform. They are of the opinion that America's march toward a fiscal abyss is a function of the disintegration of the *character* of the average American—and that we cannot expect improved conduct in Washington until we rebuild the character of those who walk on Main Street.

There is considerable truth to the notion that our collective respect for private property rights has fallen dangerously low, that we willingly redistribute the fruits of our neighbor's labors in the name of compassion and use the coercive power of government to limit his use of his property.

But our slide into a collectivist mentality and our declining self-reliance are a by-product of the erosion of the institutional and legal strictures that have led to an all-powerful, fiscally irresponsible central government. Washington covets and nurtures such popular dependence, which is essential for its preeminence. This is but another aspect of the vicious circle of government power. I am confident we can break the cycle with constitutional reform. Repairing the rupture in our governmental institutions will create an environment in which the rebuilding of individual character and self-reliance will be given an enormous boost.

POINT OF NO RETURN

But we can't wait much longer for the people's will to be done. We are approaching the "point of no return" in terms of the growth of government. For that reason there is a premium on controlling government's growth—and reversing the growth process—quickly, while it is still possible to do so. It is urgent that we act now.

More than 50 percent of the people in this country receive all or part of their income from the federal government—either directly through employment by Washington, or indirectly through a federally-funded state or local government program, or as an employee of a government contractor, or as a recipient of social security, other retirement benefits, farm subsidies, veterans benefits, welfare, various low-interest loans, unemployment compensation, or the myriad of other ways that Washington has of creating dependency. A majority have become *dependent* on the federal government.

DEPENDENCY—THE BUREAUCRATS' BEST FRIEND

That's exactly what the bureaucracy loves—for us to be dependent on them. That's the best job insurance a bureaucrat has. The more who are dependent on the federal government, the more there are with a vested personal interest in perpetuating or enlarging the federal structure.

Fortunately, a good percentage of those who receive something from Washington still view themselves primarily as tax *payers* rather than as tax *recipients*. We must move swiftly to reverse the growth of government before this view changes, making reform virtually impossible.

The cornerstone of this "noble experiment in self government" is the notion that the people are the source of all power and the arbiters of their own destiny. Supremacy of the people is maintained by carefully constraining— through the medium of our written Constitution—the powers of those whom we elect and appoint. Through the amendment process—wisely included by the Framers of the Constitution—the people may reassert that supremacy whenever their sovereignty is threatened or errors in the design of our governmental structure are revealed through the evolution of the political process.

Clearly we have arrived at such a point in our political history. What better time to "correct errors," as our Founders exhorted us to do, than during our bicentennial celebration of the framing of the document we revere. The question is not whether we ought to change the Constitution; the evidence is overwhelming that we must. The question is what happens if we fail to make changes when it is clear that there is no alternative?

POSTSCRIPT 1
SETTING PRIORITIES

To avoid a purely random outcome in trimming federal functions, we need a reasonable framework within which to weigh the relative merits of the federal government's programs and decide which should stay and which must go. This is necessary not only financially but managerially; we simply must reduce the size and scope of the federal government so it can be controlled, once again, by those we elect. Otherwise, we are doomed to being governed by the unelected staffs and bureaucrats who thrive in Washington's management twilight.

There are three ways to test the propriety of federal government activities, with some objectivity, in an effort to set priorities:

FIRST: A practical necessity test—What are those functions which by the nature of things only a government with broad national or federal scope can perform? (A Federalism analysis.)

SECOND: A requirements/values test—Whether the federal government is constitutionally or contractually bound to perform the function and, in performing it, does the federal government remain a neutral party or does it promote one set of values over another.

THIRD: A performance test—Has the function been performed effectively, efficiently and free of waste, fraud and corruption, or whether it is intrinsically susceptible to abuse.

THE PRACTICAL NECESSITY TEST

It is impractical for any individual, business organization or state/local government to defend the entire nation, engage in diplomatic interchange with foreign countries, provide international security, etc. These functions are clearly the province of a central government. So, too, are the printing of a common currency, maintenance of federally-owned lands, parks and monuments and buildings, and the operation of the federal justice system. Veterans affairs, defense-related atomic energy and space exploration, federal employee affairs, operations of Congress, the federal courts and the White House, the tax-collection function are all inherently dischargeable only by a government national in scope. While certain planning aspects of an interstate road network and air transportation system may be appropriate functions of the federal government, the execution of the plan can be done at some other level of government or privately.

A review of the federal budget by function and subfunction suggests that the activities noted above exhaust the functions which "the practical necessity test" imposes on the federal government. (Interestingly, "federalism" dictates a similar outcome in terms of the "division of labor" between Washington and other levels of government.)

THE REQUIREMENTS/VALUES TEST

We can approach this test by considering two distinct questions:

(1) What legal requirements underpin various federal functions?

(2) What role does the federal government play in carrying out such functions?

In considering the first question, the range of legal requirements would seem to be:

(a) a requirement imposed by the Constitution itself;

(b) a requirement imposed by contract validly entered into between the federal government and others;

(c) *a requirement that is purely discretionary—it may be embodied in federal statute, but that statute may be repealed (or not renewed) at will.*

With respect to the second question, the range of roles of the federal government with respect to its various programs would seem to be:

(a) *a role that is neutral—as a referee between competing interests;*

(b) *a role that involves redistribution of wealth and income to activities that are largely ideologically neutral;*

(c) *a role that involves financing programs that advance specific political, economic, social and philosophical ideas and values at the expense of others.*

These criteria lend themselves to a simple chart—federal function/role analysis—on which we can array a representative cross-section of current activities of the federal government (see Chart 2).

THE PERFORMANCE TEST

Another way to analyze federal functions is to apply performance criteria. In 1981, the National Tax Limitation Committee distributed a book entitled "Meeting America's Economic Crisis: A 'Road Map' to Emergency Federal Spending Reductions" to Senators and Representatives with the hope that they might utilize the performance criteria as a "road map" to establish priorities. Congress has given plenty of lip service to these recommendations, as it has to the Heritage Foundation's "Mandate for Leadership" and to the Grace Commission's report, but not much has been done to actually implement them.

The performance criteria, nevertheless, constitute another evaluative tool by which federal programs and activities can be compared and prioritized. The performance criteria are:

1. *proneness to fraud and abuse;*
2. *proneness to error, inefficiency and waste;*
3. *conflict or lack of coordination with other programs;*
4. *failure to satisfy cost-benefit criteria;*
5. *unjustified expansions of benefit eligibility;*
6. *lack of uniform national benefit;*
7. *impractical/unattainable program goals;*
8. *programs best performed by state, local or private agencies.*

When applied to some representative federal programs and activities, the performance criteria produce the results shown on Chart 3.

APPLYING THE TESTS TO SET PRIORITIES

Those federal functions which violate a majority of the criteria in Chart 3, which are not federal in nature under the "practical necessity test," or which qualify for "boxes" 8 or 9 in the "requirements/values test" in Chart 2 are prime candidates for elimination from Washington's Christmas tree of goodies.

BALANCING THE 1989 BUDGET

Now we come to the moment of truth. Remember at the beginning of the book I suggested that once we as a nation paid for national defense, including veterans obligations; foreign affairs and international security; contractual and quasi-contractual (trust fund) obligations such as social security, medicare, government employee retirement, etc.; interest on the national debt; and general government operations, there is no money left. Fiscal year 1989 demonstrates that clearly.

Chart 2

Requirements/Values Test

Federal Function/Role Analysis

	Gov't. role is *value neutral*—as a referee between competing interests	Gov't. role involves a redistribution of wealth but for activities which are *largely value neutral*	Gov't. role involves financing activities that *advance specific political, economic, social, and philosophical values at the expense of others*
Functions required by the *U.S. Constitution*	1 National defense Foreign policy International security & trade General gov't. (courts, national museums, etc.)	2	3

	4	5	6
Functions required by contact or other enforceable obligations	Interest on the national debt	Federal military & civilian pensions Social security* and Medicare payments Veterans benefits (some) Highway, air transportation, and unemployment insurance trust funds—taxes collected and dedicated to specific uses	
	7	8	9
Functions established by changeable or repealable laws and regulations (*discretionary*)		Farm subsidies Urban development grants Student loans Job training programs Housing subsidies Medical research	Legal services Welfare Family plng./abortion Grants for arts, humanities, political action groups

(This list is meant to be representative, not exhaustive.)

* While the specific levels of benefits are subject to congressional action, there is a general understanding—a quasi-contract—that employee-employer contributions to the system give rise to a "vested right" to retirement income.

Chart 3

Federal Program Performance Analysis*

Federal Program	1	2	3	4	5	6	7	8
Foreign assistance grants & loans	x	x	x	x	x		x	
US contributions to multilateral development banks	x	x	x	x	x		x	
Food for Peace program	x	x	x	x	x		x	
Export–Import Bank	x	x	x	x	x		x	
Farm price support and stabilization policies		x	x	x	x	x		
Economic Development Admin.	x	x	x	x	x	x	x	x
Small Business Admin.	x	x	x	x	x	x	x	x
Minority Business Development Agency	x	x	x	x	x	x	x	x
Community Development block grants	x	x	x	x	x	x	x	x
Amtrak Subsidy		x		x		x	x	x
National Inst. of Education		x	x	x			x	x
National Foundation on the Arts and the Humanities		x	x	x	x	x	x	x
Community Services Admin.	x	x	x	x	x	x	x	x
Food stamp eligibility requirement	x	x	x	x	x			
Benefit, grant, and loan programs for post-secondary students	x	x	x	x	x			x
Trade Adjustment Assistance program		x	x	x	x	x	x	x

* The numbers 1 through 8 refer to the performance criteria set forth above. The more "x"s a program scores, the more performance criteria it violates and, hence, the lower priority for continued federal funding.

Anticipated revenues in the President's budget proposal for Fiscal Year 1989 (which commenced October 1, 1988) were approximately $965 Billion, while outlays were calculated at over $1095 Billion. (The projected deficit was $130 Billion.) We'll use the revenue projections for our exercise.

Applying our tests and prioritization criteria, we have endeavored to fashion a budget for FY-1989 that is in balance with *anticipated revenues. To make sense of the federal budget for our purposes, it has been necessary to re-categorize various expenditures, pulling pieces from a variety of departments and functions and putting them in logically-linked categories. That requires some estimates and even modest guesses. I'm sure some of the categories are off by a billion or so—but as the pundits say, "that's not bad for government work." Here is what the 1989 budget might have looked like if outlays had been limited to $965 Billion of receipts (see Chart 4).*

The components of this budget design consist of the following:

• *National Defense: There has been tremendous criticism of the defense budget—the $600 toilet seats and all the rest. No doubt, the defense budget is bloated. As we have seen, members of Congress use the Defense Department, including its proliferation of bases, its weapons acquisition and development contracts, as a huge source of porkbarreling. That's the current reality. We can do better with longer-term project funding, more competitive bidding, etc. But without the discipline of the marketplace, and in the absence of true competition, it is hard to know what costs are honest and which may be terribly inflated. As a recent Heritage Foundation publication indicates, ". . . There is no known way to measure productivity in government . . ."[3]*

Also, as General Daniel O. Graham of High Frontier has pointed out, implementation of the Strategic Defense Initiative (SDI) will give us a defense against Soviet and other missile threats, rendering unnecessary many of the incredibly expensive offensive nuclear systems we're now buying: "Deployment of strategic defenses is one military program the Congress should support, not grudgingly, but enthusiastically for once a decision to <u>deploy</u> is made a number of very expensive offensive nuclear systems can be scaled back or cancelled . . . Congress will have to ask itself whether it isn't better to have a far stronger deterrent to nuclear war and save billions of dollars or stay in the costly all-offensive rut it currently finds itself. And it will have to ask if

Chart 4

FY 1989 Balanced Budget

Receipts		$965 bil.
Outlays (On- and Off-Budget)		
National defense		
President's defense proposal	286	
Defense-related space and technology	7	
Atomic energy defense activities and strategic petroleum reserve	9	
Veterans obligations	30	
	332	$332
Foreign affairs and international security (including foreign affairs-related funds appropriated to the President)	26	26
Contractual obligations for specific activities— trust funds (specific tax proceeds shared with state/local governments/others for these specific purposes):		
Unemployment insurance (portion returned to states)	17	
Transportation—highway and air transportation	18	
Miscellaneous	2	
	37	37
Contractual obligations to individuals—trust funds:		
Social security (including disability insurance trust fund)	235	
Medicare	84	
Federal employee retirement and disability	49	
	368	368
Interest on national debt, net	152	152
General government operations:		
Executive (less international security portion), Congress, Judiciary	6	
Administration of justice:	10	
Management of federal lands, resources, environment	12	
Treasury-related functions	14	
General adminstration and independent agencies	8	
		50
		$965

spending $30 billion on military systems which would reduce the damage to the country and save millions of lives should deterrence fail, is better than remaining with a far more costly program that allowed all Soviet missiles a free ride to their targets." [4]

In compiling the national defense portion of this budget, we have included the current defense budget as proposed by the President, the defense-related space and technology operations of NASA, the atomic-energy defense activities and strategic petroleum reserve of the Department of Energy budget and obligations to veterans of past wars.

• *Foreign Affairs and International Security.* Included are the budget of the State Department and those funds appropriated to the President for the support of the Agency for International Development, the CIA and other clearly foreign-affairs-related activities. I would be the last to suggest that many of these functions have been performed efficiently or that the Peace Corps is necessarily vital to the security interests of the United States. A State Department that would allow the American Embassy in Moscow to be constructed with multiple "bugs" in every room certainly suggests inefficiency and bad management.

• *Contractual Obligations for Specific Activities (trust funds).* The federal government operates several trust funds into which the proceeds of specific taxes (akin to user fees) are poured. These funds are dedicated to specific uses and are allocated to states and local units of government for the earmarked purposes. Principal among these are the unemployment insurance funds. (Included in this outlay is only that portion of unemployment taxes actually anticipated to be returned to the states); and the highway and air transportation funds. By law, these funds must be used for the dedicated purposes. This is not to suggest that when used, these funds are efficiently employed. Let's take the air traffic situation. Near misses, delays, congestion, are constantly in the news. This is clear evidence of the inability of *governmentally-generated services to keep up with the private sector. In a world of airline deregulation, the airlines have moved rapidly to develop the hub concept, to engage in fare competition and to do the other things that have led to dramatic and rapid increases in passenger miles. Only the government-provided portion of the airline industry—the air control system—has fallen woefully behind. And it's not because the funds aren't there. There's actually a surplus in the trust fund. (That's not real money, mind you, but Treasury bills, because the federal government has "borrowed" the trust funds for other purposes.) Clearly what is needed is to privatize the system by either having a federally-chartered "airways corporation" owned by the various users or participants, as Bob Poole, Chairman of Reason Foundation, has suggested,[5] or simply allow the users to contract out with private companies that provide air traffic control services on a competitive basis.*

The inefficiencies and excesses of the allocation of other transportation funds for mass transit, highway construction, etc., are well known. This pool of funds has become one of the great porkbarrel sources in the federal government.[6] Local governments often consider these funds "free money," which simply means that they are used to finance projects which, if they had to be paid for locally, would never be launched. Furthermore, every contract that is let is at the highest possible cost, because of the Davis-Bacon Act requirement to pay "prevailing" (union) wages.

• Contractual Obligations to Individuals (trust funds). Social security payments make up the bulk of this category. We must make these payments because we have a contractual, or at least quasi-contractual, obligation to those who have contributed to the system. Many of our elderly have come to rely on social security almost exclusively for their survival. Equally important to our seniors is the government-operated medical program—Medicare. We have entered an era of vast uncertainty for both senior citizens and their children in terms of increasing life

spans and unanticipated, huge medical costs for standard medical care, as well as nursing and convalescent home care.

Much has been written about the generation gap and combat that is in the offing between older people and younger workers. Before we reach that crisis point, we simply must, in a calm and dispassionate fashion, reform these programs. For example, social security expert Peter Ferrara has developed a proposal for "super-IRAs." Through a combination of private alternatives and tax credits, individuals and families can create much greater retirement income and wealth than they can achieve through the social security system, at the same contribution levels.[7] In the meantime, however, and during any period of conversion to a non-governmental system, the contractual commitments and moral obligation to our seniors must be a top priority of the federal government.

Payments to retired federal employees are contractual obligations of our government—and, hence, all of us as taxpayers. Unfortunately, there is an enormous unfunded liability to these retirees, since neither their nor the government's annual contribution comes close to providing actuarially adequate funding to meet future pension commitments. Pensions have been increasing at a greater rate than the salaries of existing employees because of generous cost-of-living adjustments (COLAs). Pension plans available to taxpayers in the private sector rarely equal those we extend to public servants. Major reform is necessary here, as well. But while such reforms are under way, the commitments remain.

• _Interest on the National Debt._ Clearly, the government of the United States must pay the interest on the debt which is held by the public, lest the government default and the full faith and credit of the government is placed in doubt. Such payments are known as "net" interest. That is the amount used in our computations for the FY 1989 budget. The difference between the net and the gross interest is by and large monies due to various trust funds operated by the federal government which hold T-bills and *other federal government obligations. In any private system, interest on such funds would have to be deposited. Under federal government "sleight-of-hand" fiscal practices, this kind of discipline is neither demanded nor provided. Therefore, as the social security trust fund has begun to build a positive balance, not only are the excess funds withdrawn or "borrowed" to pay for other current operating costs of the federal government, but the interest which would otherwise accrue on funds held in the social security account will never actually be paid. If the same rules which Congress has imposed on private pension funds, through ERISA and other fiduciary responsibility laws, were imposed on members of the House and Senate, and on others who manage federal trust funds, they would all be in jail.*

• General Government Operations. These functions include the operation of the White House and the President's staff, Congress and the court system; the Justice Department, the FBI, the U.S. attorney system throughout the Nation and the variety of penal institutions and other federal law enforcement activities; the management of public lands, parks, monuments, resources and some environmental programs; Department of the Treasury-related functions, including the Mint, Federal Reserve System, Internal Revenue Service, etc.; and general government administration, including the operation of independent agencies. No doubt there is plenty of room for improvement in the operation and efficiency of many of these departments and programs, but they do represent what we generally consider to be the basic elements of the federal government.

SUMMARY: There you have it. Those are the federal functions for which funds were available. The harsh reality is that a balanced budget in FY-1989 left no money for subsidies, grants to the arts, energy research, redevelopment in the cities or for federally-sponsored education, welfare, non-Medicare health activities, etc. This is not merely my conclusion. You cannot "slay the messenger" in the hope that the message will go away or will get any better. The numbers dictate the outcome. But that is not the end of it. In order to absorb *"unexpected"* expenditures, such as the savings and loan bailouts, student loan defaults and additional Medicare costs, it is essential that we streamline the operations of each *"surviving"* function of government.

POSTSCRIPT 2
CONGRESSIONAL REFORM AMENDMENT

An amendment to the United States Constitution containing the following provisions should help restore the Congress to the institution that was envisioned by the Founders:

1 (Terms:) Service in the Senate of the United States shall be limited to two terms and in the House of Representatives to four terms; but in no event shall any person serve in the Congress of the United States for more than 12 years, except to complete an unexpired term in the United States Senate.

2 (Compensation:) Members of Congress shall be compensated for each day they are in attendance at a regular session of Congress, or at a special session as may be called by the President; the daily amount of compensation and expenses shall be determined by a recorded roll call vote of each house of Congress and shall be effective commencing with the next Congress; there shall be no pensions or other form of compensation to members of Congress following their service; there shall be no limitation on the occupation or non-congressional income of members of Congress.

3 (Regular Sessions of Congress:) Congress shall meet in regular session not more than six consecutive days per month, which shall be consecutive, unless called into special session by the President.

4 (Statutes:) Congress may not exempt itself from the effect or operation of any law which it shall approve.

PART IV

SETTING
NEW LIMITS

CHAPTER 14

THE CONSTITUTIONAL SOLUTION

I wish it were possible to obtain a single amendment to our Constitution. I would be willing to depend on that alone for the reduction of the administration of our government to the genuine principles of its constitution; I mean an additional article, taking from the federal government the power of borrowing.

(*Thomas Jefferson*)[1]

WHEN Jefferson expressed concern about federal borrowing, the Constitution prohibited direct taxes on states, companies, or individuals. There was a built-in tax limitation on the federal government whose revenues were restricted to trade duties, imposts, fees, etc. Hence, a restraint on borrowing (a balanced budget provision), together with the extant prohibition against direct taxes, would have constituted an effective limitation on the size of federal spending. Jefferson's concerns extended not only to fiscally responsible and frugal government but to the size, power, and intrusiveness of government, as well. "That government which governs least, governs best," he said.

Were Jefferson alive today (or any time after passage of the Sixteenth [income tax] Amendment in 1913), it is likely he would have expanded his amendment to include a limitation on federal taxes, as well as borrowing, thereby controlling total spending—and the size and power of the federal government.

CRITERIA FOR AMENDING THE CONSTITUTION

Amending the Constitution of the United States is a serious matter. Those of us who care deeply about the American heritage of liberty and justice for all must address this responsibility with utmost respect. Before undertaking it, we should be satisfied beyond all reasonable doubt that the following criteria have been met:

- there exists a structural, long-observed defect in the functioning of the federal government and that it is of such severity as to pose a clear danger to the welfare of the country (such as the spending "bias" of the federal government that has promoted grossly excessive federal taxation and deficits, risking the economic health of the Republic);

- there is no prospect the defect will either go away in time or be corrected by means other than a constitutional amendment (a long series of statutory measures to balance the budget have been tried and have not corrected the problem);

- the proposed amendment is formulated to correct the defect (constitutional scholars, legal experts, and sitting members of the House and Senate have all contributed to the development of the tax limitation/balanced budget amendment); and

- the proposed amendment is fully within the constitutional tradition and in harmony with the existing body and intent of the Constitution (the clear intent of the Constitution and the Bill of Rights is to *limit* federal powers in order to ensure individual freedom. The tax limitation/balanced budget amendment is very much within this tradition and seeks to *limit* abusive federal taxing and spending powers).

Questions about the objectives of and need for such an amendment are dealt with in greater detail in Postscript 1 to this chapter.

AMENDMENT DESIGN— ESSENTIAL ELEMENTS

Merely passing an amendment is not enough. Attention to the design of the amendment is crucial. While there is no *perfect* amendment—because reasonable people can disagree about such things—there are design elements that *are* important.

- An amendment should require that the federal government operate on a balanced budget. We should not pass forward to future generations a burden of debt. The balance need not be yearly; in fact, it is very difficult to achieve balance each and every year. That requires "shooting" at two moving targets simultaneously— expenditures and revenues. Each can change unexpectedly. It is vital that the balance requirement of the amendment be firm but flexible.

• An amendment must also place a limit on the growth rate of taxes and spending. The preferred design is to limit taxes so that they grow no faster than the growth rate of the general economy, as measured by national income growth.

• An amendment should prevent budgetary sleight of hand. It should control *all* outlays so that Congress may not defeat this discipline by so-called "off-budget" expenditures. It should accommodate biennial budgeting and other improvements in the federal budget process.

• Flexibility to meet wartime needs and true emergency situations is an important amendment feature. In time of declared war, the amendment would be suspended. At all other times, the limits set by the amendment could be exceeded for *only a single year* upon a super-majority vote of Congress to meet an "emergency." (Rather than try to define an "emergency," which is often in the eye of the beholder, it is preferable to let the political process "define" it by virtue of a super-majority vote.)

Several different amendment designs are set forth in Postscript 2 to this chapter.

POSTSCRIPT 1

QUESTIONS AND ANSWERS REGARDING A CONSTITUTIONAL SOLUTION

QUESTION: *What is the objective and purpose of the tax limitation/balanced budget amendment?*

ANSWER: *The objective of the amendment was stated well by the Senate Judiciary Committee:*

> *In proposing (the amendment), the Committee seeks to re-establish constitutional limitations upon federal spending and deficit practices that existed in earlier years . . . Specifically, the proposed amendment addresses a serious spending bias in the present fiscal process arising from the fact that Members of Congress do not have to cast votes in behalf of new taxes in order to accommodate new spending programs. Rather than having to cast such politically disadvantageous votes, they may either resort to increased levels of deficit spending or allow the tax system, through 'bracket creep,' to produce annual, automatic tax increases.*
>
> *Members of Congress, thus, are free to respond to the concentrated pressures of spending interest groups—and reap the political advantages of doing so—without having to reap the concomitant political disadvantages by reducing spending programs favored by some other spending interests or expressly raising taxes.*
>
> *The result is that spending continues inexorably to rise whatever the genuine will of the people. The result is an essentially undemocratic and unresponsive process that enables Members of Congress to avoid ultimate accountability for their spending and taxing decisions. It is the existence of this bias that convinces the Committee that a constitutional solution is now required.*"[2]

QUESTION: *Why not simply pass a law to limit spending, taxes and deficits instead of amending the Constitution?*

ANSWER: *It has been tried over and over and just doesn't work. Balanced budgets have, in fact, been required by law since 1979, but we haven't even come close to a balanced budget. The Budget Control Act of 1974, designed by Congress as a means of disciplining itself, is in a shambles. Gramm-Rudman-Hollings (GRH) has been honored in the breach, repaired, ignored, debated, avoided. It has helped, but the Founding Fathers were right. Statutory limitations never succeed for the simple reason that congress is not bound by its own decisions. Only the Constitution can effectively limit Congress.*

QUESTION: Are the issues addressed by the amendment suitable for the Constitution?

ANSWER: Absolutely. The Constitution itself provides for an amending process to address structural flaws that develop in the functioning of the government, such as the "spending bias" we are trying to correct. The amendment seeks a fiscally-responsible and constitutionally-sound remedy for this defect. It is fully in harmony with the original and enduring purposes of the Constitution and, in fact, acts to restore constitutional limitations of federal power that have been eroded by bad tax laws and dishonest monetary practices.

Says Dr. Milton Friedman,

> The amendment is very much in the spirit of the Bill of Rights, the first ten amendments to the Constitution. Their purpose was to limit government in order to free the people. Similarly, the purpose of the Tax Limitation/Balanced Budget Amendment is to limit the government in order to free the people, in this instance from excessive taxation.
>
> It is no surprise that a torrent of criticism has been loosed against the proposed amendment by people who believe that our problems arise not from excessive government but from the failure to give government enough power, or enough control over us as individuals.

QUESTION: How exactly does the amendment correct this "spending bias?"

ANSWER: The amendment limits overall spending, taxes and deficits. It creates an atmosphere in which elected officials can say "no" to the incessant demands of spending interests and thus can conduct federal business in a responsible manner. No longer will the taxpayer be the automatic loser in every spending proposal that comes down the road.

QUESTION: Won't the amendment make it impossible for Congress to respond to changing economic conditions?

ANSWER: Congress can allocate its spending as it sees fit to meet changing conditions. The amendment only sets a limit on the total. If there is a true emergency, Congress has the flexibility to meet such needs.

QUESTION: Isn't it true that the amendment imposes a particular economic system on the Nation?

ANSWER: That's nonsense, unless balanced budgets reflect a "system." If so, it is the same "economic system" that has always been part of the Constitution and which was unfailingly observed until recent decades. The amendment simply limits government's power, which is in the grand tradition of our Constitution.

QUESTION: Can Congress avoid the restraints of the amendment by spending "off budget?"

ANSWER: No. The amendment is deliberately worded to include all federal outlays, without any distinction between "on-budget" or "off-budget" items.

QUESTION: Can Congress evade the amendment with loan guarantees?

ANSWER: Yes, temporarily. Since loan guarantees are not "outlays" in the year they are made, they do not have to be budgeted. However, when and to the extent the loans are defaulted, they must be included in outlays and would, therefore, fall under the amendment provisions. Because such defaulted loans would crowd out other spending, Congress will have to be careful about making the guarantees in the first place.

QUESTION: Can Congress adjust to the constraints of the amendment by passing on some of its current functions to states, local governments and the private sector?

ANSWER: The prospect of Congress prioritizing its responsibilities in this manner is not a drawback but, rather, a huge "plus" for the amendment. Many of such chores can and should be undertaken privately, or by local government. The "closer to home" we tackle our problems, the more the solutions will be in the hands of those most familiar with the situation. Result: not only better answers, but faster, cheaper and far more efficient solutions and large net tax savings. Taking care of things at home and not sending our every little complaint to Washington for solution—along with large chunks of our paychecks to pay for it—would be an admirable habit to which to return. It used to be the American way. It will work again as well as ever.

QUESTION: The goal is to require a balanced budget. With the $100-$200 billion deficits of recent years, is this realistic?

ANSWER: By all means! The real question is, does anything less make any sense? We have had a virtual breakdown in the political process on Capitol Hill, not to mention in congressional "budgeting." Well-financed (by us!), skilled and very numerous special interest organizations have simply overwhelmed responsible government.

Our disastrous fiscal policies and enormous deficits are precisely the result of this one-sided contest. Correcting the situation is not "unrealistic" but an absolute and urgent necessity.

Those who assert that every penny cut from the federal budget is stealing bread from the poor, that fiscal restraint is somehow bad for us, that we aren't showing caring, concern and compassion—those people are engaged in big government propaganda. The Grace Commission identified 2,478 specific ways to slash the federal budget, without taking so much as a dime away from the poor. All the Commission recommendations were based on ordinary, cost-conscious business practices which could save hundreds of billions of dollars. And remember, chairman Peter Grace said, "We just scratched the surface."

QUESTION: *What if the federal deficit were to shrink and the problem "solved itself" through economic growth? Why, then, should we go to all the bother of amending the Constitution?*

ANSWER: *Nothing could please us more. But let's not kid ourselves. The "spending bias" has been around for well over a halfcentury. We must institute real and permanent reforms that will be immune to the whims of the moment—which means only one thing: a constitutional limitation on federal spending and deficits.*

QUESTION: *So the crux of the matter is permanence?*

ANSWER: *Absolutely—as well as economic stability and predictability. There is practically nothing more harmful to free and open markets—which is to say, to private exchanges, to capital investment, to job creation, to production, to economic growth and to the continuance of your income—than a stable and responsible fiscal environment. Business, on which all of our livelihoods depend, simply cannot plan or expand rationally if the future value of money, and the stability of private contracts, are subject to bureaucratic whims.*

The point is, we need a <u>permanent</u> end to tax abuse and spending "unlimited." "Easy-come, easy-go" federal policies ultimately harm everyone, even the big spenders, and have to be curtailed on a permanent basis. Only the tax limitation/balanced budget amendment can do this now.

QUESTION: *When will the amendment take effect?*

ANSWER: *It will take effect for the second fiscal year after its ratification by the states.*

QUESTION: Wouldn't passage of the amendment trigger a depression? Millions of people will lose part or all of their federal paychecks, and thousands of companies would lose government contracts.

ANSWER: Money that the federal government neither borrows nor takes in taxes remains in the hands of those who produce it. They are more careful and efficient in its use. Those dollars are more "powerful" than if they were spent by government. The result would be a stronger economy and nation, not a weaker one.

QUESTION: Wouldn't Congress be guilty of hypocrisy in voting for a large federal deficit, while simultaneously approving a constitutional amendment to prevent future deficits?

ANSWER: Dr. Milton Friedman provides an incisive response:

> *I have long believed that congressional hypocrisy and short-sightedness are the only reasons there is a ghost of a chance of getting Congress to pass an amendment limiting itself. Most members of Congress will do anything to postpone the problems they face by a couple of years—only Wall Street has a shorter perspective. If the hypocrisy did not exist, if Congress behaved responsibly, there would be no need for the amendment. Congress' irresponsibility is the reason we need an amendment and at the same time is the reason there is a chance of getting one.*
>
> *Hypocrisy may eventually lead to the passing of the amendment. But hypocrisy will not prevent the amendment from having important effects three or four years down the line—and from casting its shadow on events even earlier. Congress will not violate the Constitution lightly. Members of Congress will wriggle and squirm; they will seek, and no doubt find, subterfuges and evasions. But their actions will be significantly affected by the existence of the amendment. The experience of several states that have passed similar tax limitation amendments provides ample evidence of that.*

QUESTION: What makes you believe that a fiscal amendment will actually control and reduce taxes, spending and deficits. What evidence do you have?

ANSWER: We have known it from experience, intuition and common sense. Now, however, we have a definitive study on the topic. The highly-respected Advisory Commission on Intergovernmental Relations (ACIR) has completed an exhaustive analysis of the constitutional fiscal restraints in <u>each and every</u> state in the Union—comparing taxing, spending, debt and deficit-creation experiences as between the various states.

The ACIR study concluded that strong constitutional balanced budget and other limitation requirements significantly reduced spending, taxes and debt. Specifically, it reported these major results:

1) there is a significant correlation between more stringent balanced budget requirements and smaller deficits (and larger surpluses); 2) there is a significant correlation between more stringent balanced budget requirements and lower levels of state spending; 3) there is a significant correlation between more stringent balanced budget requirements and lower levels of state tax burden; 4) there is a possibly significant relationship between the presence of state level Tax and Expenditure Limitations and lower state spending; 5) there is a possibly significant relationship between the presence of a state constitutional debt restriction and lower levels of state debt in various forms; 6) there is a significant relationship between the magnitude of the governor's veto activity and lower levels of state spending; 7) there is a significant relationship between the magnitude of the governor's veto activity and lower levels of state economic regulation; and 8) there is a possibly significant relationship between the stringency of a state's balanced budget requirement and the rate of economic growth in the state over the 1970's, with states having more stringent balanced budget requirements also having higher rates of economic growth.[2]

The study concludes that similar fiscal restraints on the federal government should produce the same kinds of results in Washington.

QUESTION: What makes you think the amendment would be

enforced? Won't Congress find ways to circumvent the constraints of the amendment?

ANSWER: Of course, the liberal big spenders will endeavor to subvert the operation of the amendment. But there would be substantial political risk associated with votes to unbalance the budget or to increase the rate of tax and spending growth. These would be highly visible roll-call votes. NTLC and other taxpayer lobbies will play a vital role in monitoring congressional "cheating," in shaping enforcement legislation, and in blowing the whistle on every effort to circumvent the amendment.

There is a crucial, built-in enforcement safeguard. The amendment imposes a responsibility on both the Congress and the President to assure that actual outlays do not exceed those authorized under the amendment. This provision will bring into play the historic jealousy of Congress over its appropriation and budgetary authority. If federal outlays threatened to exceed the limit in a given year, prompting the President to intervene and make outlay decisions, Congress's budgetary prerogatives would be challenged. To preclude this outcome Congress will adopt those fiscal procedures most likely to achieve compliance with the amendment. Congress will find it in its own best interest to honor the amendment.

100TH CONGRESS
1ST SESSION
H. J. RES. 321

Proposing an amendment to the Constitution to provide for a balanced budget for the United States Government and for greater accountability in the enactment of tax legislation.

IN THE HOUSE OF REPRESENTATIVES

JUNE 17, 1987

Mr. STENHOLM (for himself, Mr. CRAIG, Mr. ROBERT F. SMITH, Mr. CARPER, Mr. GIBBONS, Mr. ANDERSON, Mr. ANTHONY, Mr. ARCHER, Mr. ARMEY, Mr. BADHAM, Mr. BAKER, Mr. BALLENGER, Mr. BARNARD, Mr. BARTLETT, Mr. BARTON of Texas, Mr. BATEMAN, Mr. BENNETT, Mrs. BENTLEY, Mr. BEREUTER, Mr. BEVILL, Mr. BILBRAY, Mr. BILIRAKIS, Mr. BLAZ, Mr. BLILEY, Mr. BOEHLERT, Mr. BONER of Tennessee, Mr. BOSCO, Mr. BOULTER, Mr. BROOMFIELD, Mr. BROWN of Colorado, Mr. BUECHNER, Mr. BUNNING, Mr. BURTON of Indiana, Mr. BUSTAMANTE, Mrs. BYRON, Mr. CALLAHAN, Mr. CAMPBELL, Mr. CHANDLER, Mr. CHAPMAN, Mr. CHAPPELL, Mr. CHENEY, Mr. CLARKE, Mr. CLINGER, Mr. COATS, Mr. COBLE, Mr. COLEMAN of Missouri, Mr. COMBEST, Mr. COURTER, Mr. CRANE, Mr. DANIEL, Mr. DANNEMEYER, Mr. DARDEN, Mr. DAUB, Mr. DAVIS of Illinois, Mr. DAVIS of Michigan, Mr. DE LA GARZA, Mr. DELAY, Mr. DERRICK, Mr. DEWINE, Mr. DICKINSON, Mr. DIOGUARDI, Mr. DORGAN of North Dakota, Mr. DORNAN of California, Mr. DOWDY of Mississippi, Mr. DREIER of California, Mr. DUNCAN, Mr. DYSON, Mr. EDWARDS of Oklahoma, Mr. EMERSON, Mr. ENGLISH, Mr. ERDREICH, Mr. ESPY, Mr. FAWELL, Mr. FIELDS, Mr. FLIPPO, Mr. FRENZEL, Mr. GALLEGLY, Mr. GALLO, Mr. GEKAS, Mr. GINGRICH, Mr. GOODLING, Mr. GORDON, Mr. GRANDY, Mr. GRANT, Mr. GREGG, Mr. GUNDERSON, Mr. HALL of Texas, Mr. HAMMERSCHMIDT, Mr. HANSEN, Mr. HARRIS, Mr. HASTERT, Mr. HATCHER, Mr. HEFLEY, Mr. HEFNER, Mr. HENRY, Mr. HERGER, Mr. HILER, Mr. HOLLOWAY, Mr. HOPKINS, Mr. HORTON, Mr. HUBBARD, Mr. HUCKABY, Mr. HUNTER, Mr. HUTTO, Mr. INHOFE, Mr. IRELAND, Mr. JACOBS, Mr. JENKINS, Mrs. JOHNSON of Connecticut, Mr. JOHNSON of South Dakota, Mr. JONES of Tennessee, Mr. JONES of North Carolina, Mr. KASICH, Mr. KOLBE, Mr. KONNYU, Mr. KYL, Mr. LAGOMARSINO, Mr. LANCASTER, Mr. LATTA, Mr. LEACH of Iowa, Mr. LEATH of Texas, Mr. LENT, Mr. LEWIS of California, Mr. LEWIS of Florida, Mr. LIGHTFOOT, Mr. LIVINGSTON, Mrs. LLOYD, Mr. LOTT, Mr. LOWERY of California, Mr. LUJAN, Mr. THOMAS A. LUKEN, Mr. DONALD E. LUKENS, Mr. LUNGREN, Mr. MCCANDLESS, Mr. MCCOLLUM, Mr. MCCURDY, Mr. MCDADE, Mr.

McEwen, Mr. McGrath, Mr. McMillan of North Carolina, Mr. McMillen of Maryland, Mr. Mack, Mr. MacKay, Mr. Madigan, Mr. Marlenee, Mr. Martin of New York, Mrs. Martin of Illinois, Mrs. Meyers of Kansas, Mr. Michel, Mr. Miller of Ohio, Mr. Miller of Washington, Mr. Molinari, Mr. Montgomery, Mr. Moorhead, Mr. Morrison of Washington, Mr. Neal, Mr. Nelson of Florida, Mr. Nichols, Mr. Nielson of Utah, Mr. Ortiz, Mr. Owens of Utah, Mr. Oxley, Mr. Packard, Mr. Parris, Mrs. Patterson, Mr. Penny, Mr. Petri, Mr. Pickle, Mr. Porter, Mr. Price of North Carolina, Mr. Pursell, Mr. Quillen, Mr. Ravenel, Mr. Ray, Mr. Regula, Mr. Richardson, Mr. Ridge, Mr. Ritter, Mr. Roberts, Mr. Robinson, Mr. Roemer, Mr. Rogers, Mr. Rose, Mr. Roth, Mr. Rowland of Connecticut, Mr. Rowland of Georgia, Mrs. Saiki, Mr. Saxton, Mr. Schaefer, Mr. Schuette, Mr. Schulze, Mr. Sensenbrenner, Mr. Shaw, Mr. Shumway, Mr. Shuster, Mr. Skeen, Mr. Skelton, Mr. Slaughter of Virginia, Mr. Smith of New Jersey, Mr. Denny Smith, Mr. Smith of Texas, Mr. Smith of New Hampshire, Mrs. Smith of Nebraska, Ms. Snowe, Mr. Solomon, Mr. Spence, Mr. Stallings, Mr. Stangeland, Mr. Stump, Mr. Sundquist, Mr. Sweeney, Mr. Swindall, Mr. Tallon, Mr. Tauke, Mr. Taylor, Mr. Tauzin, Mr. Thomas of California, Mr. Upton, Mr. Valentine, Mr. Vander Jagt, Mr. Volkmer, Mrs. Vucanovich, Mr. Walker, Mr. Watkins, Mr. Weber, Mr. Weldon, Mr. Whittaker, Mr. Wilson, Mr. Wolf, Mr. Wortley, Mr. Wylie, Mr. Young of Alaska, and Mr. Young of Florida) introduced the following joint resolution; which was referred to the Committee on the Judiciary

JOINT RESOLUTION

Proposing an amendment to the Constitution to provide for a balanced budget for the United States Government and for greater accountability in the enactment of tax legislation.

1   *Resolved by the Senate and House of Representatives*

2   *of the United States of America in Congress assembled*

3   *(two-thirds of each House concurring therein)*, That the fol-

4   lowing article is proposed as an amendment to the Constitu-

5   tion of the United States, which shall be valid to all intents

6   and purposes as part of the Constitution if ratified by the

1 legislatures of three-forths of the several States within seven
2 years after its submission to the States for ratification:

3   "ARTICLE —

4   "SECTION 1. Prior to each fiscal year, the Congress and
5 the President shall agree on an estimate of total receipts for
6 that fiscal year by enactment into law of a joint resolution
7 devoted solely to that subject. Total outlays for that year
8 shall not exceed the level of estimated receipts set forth in
9 such joint resolution, unless three-fifths of the total member-
10 ship of each House of Congress shall provide, by a rollcall
11 vote, for a specific excess of outlays over estimated receipts.

12   "SECTION 2. Whenever actual outlays exceed actual re-
13 ceipts for any fiscal year, the Congress shall, in the ensuing
14 fiscal year, provide by law for the repayment of such excess.
15 The public debt of the United States shall not be increased
16 unless three-fifths of the total membership of each House
17 shall provide by law for such an increase by a rollcall vote.

18   "SECTION 3. Prior to each fiscal year, the President
19 shall transmit to the Congress a proposed budget for the
20 United States Government for that fiscal year in which total
21 outlays do not exceed total receipts.

22   "SECTION 4. No bill to increase revenue shall become
23 law unless approved by a majority of the total membership of
24 each House by a rollcall vote.

1   "SECTION 5. The provisions of this article are waived

2 for any fiscal year in which a declaration of war is in effect.

3   "SECTION 6. Total receipts shall include all receipts of

4   the United States except those derived from borrowing. Total

5   outlays shall include all outlays of the United States except

6 for those for repayment of debt principal.

7   "SECTION 7. This article shall take effect beginning

8 with fiscal year 1991 or with the second fiscal year beginning

9 after its ratification, whichever is later.".

O

101st CONGRESS
1st SESSION

S. J. RES. 2

Proposing an amendment to the Constitution relating to a Federal balanced budget and tax limitation.

IN THE SENATE OF THE UNITED STATES

JANUARY 25 (legislative day, JANUARY 3), 1989

Mr. DOLE (for himself, Mr. THURMOND, Mr. HATCH, Mr. BOND, Mr. BOSCH-WITZ, Mr. BURNS, Mr. COCHRAN, Mr. HELMS, Mr. KASTEN, Mr. MCCAIN, Mr. MCCONNELL, Mr. ROTH, Mr. STEVENS, Mr. SYMMS, Mr. WILSON, Mr. DANFORTH, Mr. DURENBERGER, Mr. GARN, Mr. GRAMM, Mr. WALLOP, Mr. WARNER, Mr. LOTT, and Mr. MURKOWSKI) introduced the following joint resolution; which was read twice and referred to the Committee on the Judiciary

---

JOINT RESOLUTION

Proposing an amendment to the Constitution relating to a Federal balanced budget and tax limitation.

1   *Resolved by the Senate and House of Representatives*

2 *of the United States of America in Congress assembled*

3 *(two-thirds of each House concurring therein),* That the fol-

4 lowing article is proposed as an amendment to the Constitu-

5 tion of the United States, which shall be valid to all intents

6 and purposes as part of the Constitution if ratified by the

7 legislatures of three-fourths of the several States within

8 seven years after its submission to the States for ratification:

1   "Article—

2   "Section 1. Prior to each fiscal year, the Congress
3 shall adopt a statement for that year in which total outlays
4 are not greater than total receipts. The Congress may amend
5 such statement provided amended outlays are not greater
6 than amended receipts. With the approval of three-fifths of
7 the whole number of both Houses, the Congress, in such
8 statement, may provide for a specific excess of outlays over
9 receipts. Actual outlays shall not exceed the outlays set forth
10 in such statement.

11   "Section 2. Total receipts in the statement adopted
12 pursuant to this article shall not increase by a rate greater
13 than the rate of increase in national income in the previous
14 fiscal year, unless a majority of the whole number of both
15 Houses shall have passed a bill directed solely to approving
16 specific additional receipts and such bill has become law.

17   "Section 3. The Congress may waive the provisions of
18 this article for any fiscal year in which a declaration of war is
19 in effect.

20   "Section 4. This article shall take effect for the second
21 fiscal year beginning after its ratification.".

O

101ST CONGRESS
1ST SESSION

S. J. RES. 12

Proposing an amendment to the Constitution relating to a Federal balanced budget.

IN THE SENATE OF THE UNITED STATES

JANUARY 25 (legislative day, JANUARY 3), 1989

Mr. THURMOND (for himself, Mr. HATCH, Mr. GRASSLEY, Mr. STEVENS, Mr. GARN, Mr. MCCONNELL, Mr. KASTEN, Mr. SIMPSON, Mr. COCHRAN, Mr. HELMS, Mr. GRAMM, Mr. LUGAR, Mr. DECONCINI, Mr. HUMPHREY, Mr. ROTH, Mr. SYMMS, Mr. PRESSLER, Mr. WALLOP, Mr. JOHNSTON, and Mr. D'AMATO) introduced the following joint resolution; which was read twice and referred to the Committee on the Judiciary

---

JOINT RESOLUTION

Proposing an amendment to the Constitution relating to a Federal balanced budget.

1   *Resolved by the Senate and House of Representatives*
2 *of the United States of America in Congress assembled*
3 *(two-thirds of each House concurring therein)*, That the fol-
4 lowing article is proposed as an amendment to the Constitu-
5 tion of the United States, which shall be valid to all intents
6 and purposes as part of the Constitution if ratified by the
7 legislatures of three-fourths of the several States within
8 seven years after its submission to the States for ratification:

1   "ARTICLE —

2   "SECTION 1. Total outlays of the United States for any

3   fiscal year shall not exceed total receipts to the United States

4   for that year, unless three-fifths of the whole number of both

5   Houses of Congress shall provide for a specific excess of out-

6   lays over receipts.

7   "SECTION 2. Any bill for raising taxes shall become law

8   only if approved by a majority of the whole number of both

9   Houses of Congress by rollcall vote.

10   "SECTION 3. The Congress may waive the provisions of

11 this article for any fiscal year in which a declaration of war is

12 in effect.

13   "SECTION 4. Total receipts shall include all receipts of

14 the United States except those derived from borrowing. Total

15 outlays shall include all outlays of the United States except

16 for those for repayment of debt principal.

17   "SECTION 5. This article shall take effect beginning

18 with fiscal year 1992 or with the second fiscal year beginning

19 after the ratification, whichever is later.".

O

101st CONGRESS
1st Session

S. J. RES. 30

Proposing an amendment to the Constitution relating to Federal budget
procedures.

IN THE SENATE OF THE UNITED STATES

JANUARY 25 (legislative day, JANUARY 3), 1989

Mr. GRAMM introduced the following joint resolution; which was read twice and
referred to the Committee on the Judiciary

JOINT RESOLUTION

Proposing an amendment to the Constitution relating to Federal
budget procedures.

1   *Resolved by the Senate and House of Representatives*
2 *of the United States of America in Congress assembled*
3 *(two-thirds of each House concurring therein)*, That the fol-
4 lowing article is proposed as an amendment to the Constitu-
5 tion of the United States, which shall be valid to all intents
6 and purposes as part of the Constitution if ratified by the
7 legislatures of three-fourths of the several States within
8 seven years after its submission to the States for ratification:

1   "ARTICLE —

2   "SECTION 1. Prior to each fiscal year, Congress shall
3   adopt a statement of receipts and outlays for such fiscal year
4   in which total outlays are not greater than total receipts.
5   Congress may amend such statement provided revised out-
6   lays are not greater than revised receipts. Congress may pro-
7   vide in such statement for a specific excess of outlays over
8   receipts by a vote directed solely to that subject in which
9   three-fifths of the whole number of each House agree to such
10   excess. The Congress and the President shall ensure that
11   actual outlays do not exceed the outlays set forth in such
12   statement.

13   "SECTION 2. Total receipts for any fiscal year set forth
14   in the statement adopted pursuant to the first section of this
15   article shall not increase by a rate greater than the rate of
16   increase in national income in the year or years ending not
17   less than six months before such fiscal year, unless a majority
18   of the whole number of each House of Congress shall have
19   passed a bill directed solely to approving specific additional
20   receipts and such bill has become law.

21   "SECTION 3. Prior to each fiscal year, the President
22   shall transmit to Congress a proposed statement of receipts
23   and outlays for such fiscal year consistent with the provisions
24   of this article.

1   "SECTION 4. The Congress may waive the provisions of
2 this article for any fiscal year in which a declaration of war is
3 in effect.

4   "SECTION 5. Total receipts shall include all receipts of
5 the United States except those derived from borrowing and
6 total outlays shall include all outlays of the United States
7 except those for the repayment of debt principal.

8   "SECTION 6. The amount of Federal public debt as of
9 the first day of the second fiscal year beginning after the
10 ratification of this article shall become a permanent limit on
11 such debt and there shall be no increase in such amount
12 unless three-fifths of the whole number of each House of
13 Congress shall have passed a bill approving such increase
14 and such bill has become law.

15   "SECTION 7. The Congress shall enforce and implement
16 this article by appropriate legislation.

17   "SECTION 8. This article shall take effect for the fiscal
18 year 1993 or for the second fiscal year beginning after its
19 ratification.".

○

CHAPTER 15

THE BATTLE FOR THE AMENDMENT

The simple process of preserving our present civilization is supremely complex, and demands incalculably subtle powers.

(Ortega y Gasset)

THE battle for a tax limitation/balanced budget amendment has its roots in an assignment it was my pleasure to undertake for then-California Governor Ronald Reagan during 1972 and 1973. As Chairman of the Governor's Tax Reduction Task Force, I enlisted the aid of some of the finest free-market minds in America. These experts were very concerned about the rapidly increasing share of national income that was being consumed by government at all levels. Among the advisors to the Task Force, many of whom have since served in senior policy roles for President Reagan's administration, were:

• Martin Anderson, Senior Fellow in Public Policy, The Hoover Institution, and former Assistant to the President for Policy Development;

• James Buchanan, Nobel Laureate, Economist, George Mason University, Virginia;

• Glenn Campbell, Director of The Hoover Institution; Peter Drucker, Claremont Graduate School;

• Roger A. Freeman, Senior Fellow, The Hoover Institution; Milton Friedman, Nobel Laureate, Economist, Advisor to President Reagan, and Senior Fellow at The Hoover Institution;

• C. Lowell Harriss, Professor of Economics, Columbia University;

• Anthony M. Kennedy, Justice of the Supreme Court, former Professor of Constitutional Law, McGeorge School of Law, University of the Pacific, Sacramento;

• J. Clayburn LaForce, Dean of the Graduate School of Management, UCLA;

• William A. Niskanen, Chairman, The Cato Institute, former chief economist of Ford Motor Co. and member of the President's Council of Economic Advisors, Washington, D.C.;

• Wm. Craig Stubblebine, member of the National Tax Limitation Committee's Board of Directors, Professor of Economics, Claremont McKenna College, Claremont, California;

• Norman Ture, tax consultant and economist, Washington, D.C., former Assistant Secretary of the Treasury for Tax Policy.

CALIFORNIA'S CONSTITUTIONAL SPENDING LIMIT

Together we devised the first state constitutional limit designed to ensure that taxes and spending would not grow faster than the economy. In fact, we sought an orderly reduction of the state's share of California personal income.

Proposition 1 was submitted as an initiative to the voters at a special election in November 1973 called by Governor Reagan following a successful signature drive. The measure had significant and broad-based popular support, but, unfortunately, the campaign was neither well conceived nor competently executed. Ronald Reagan was positioned as "point man" in the campaign, and his personal prestige was on the line.

All of the candidates for the 1974 Democratic gubernatorial nomination lined up against the amendment. They echoed the message of fear and doom contrived by the public education establishment, public employee unions, and other tax "consumers." Proposition 1 failed narrowly at the polls. But out of its defeat was born the National Tax Limitation Committee in 1975.

TENNESSEE ACTS FIRST

Under the guidance of State Representative David Y. Copeland, a Tennessee State Constitutional Convention proposed a tax limitation amendment. The people approved it in the Spring of 1978, making Tennessee the first state to adopt such a constitutional rule. The June 1978 victory for California's Proposition 13 (a property-tax limitation amendment) fueled an already rampant nationwide tax revolt.

Since then, numerous states have adopted tax and spending limitation measures to control government's seemingly insatiable appetite: California, Michigan, Washington, Massachusetts, Missouri, New Jersey, and South Carolina, to mention a few.

FEDERAL SPENDING LIMIT AMENDMENT

In the late summer of 1978, believing that the time had arrived to begin work at the federal level, we reconvened many members of the old Proposition 1 task force, including Milton Friedman, Bill Niskanen, Craig Stubblebine, and others. We augmented their ranks with people from other disciplines, including political science, sociology, and constitutional law. Among the "new faces" were Robert Bork and Ralph Winters, then Yale Law School professors; sociologist Robert Nisbet; Washington tax lobbyist and former Deputy Secretary of the Treasury Charls Walker; University of California, Berkeley, Political Scientist Aaron Wildavsky; economist Walter Williams; and Robert B. Carleson, member of the National Tax Limitation Committee's Board of Directors, former Policy Advisor to President Reagan and a former U.S. Commissioner of Welfare. For seven months the federal amendment drafting committee met periodically, exchanging numerous drafts of the proposed amendment. Finally, the first federal spending amendment emerged.

Introduced as Senate Joint Resolution 56 and House Joint Resolution 450 by Senators John Heinz (R-PA) and

Richard Stone (D-FL) and Representatives Barber Conable (R-NY) and Ed Jenkins (D-GA), the measure languished in a Congress whose leadership was largely hostile to the concept of tax and spending limitation. We began the arduous process of developing an institutional support base. Early to join the tax limitation/balanced budget amendment coalition were the American Farm Bureau Federation, the National Federation of Independent Business, the National Cattlemen's Association, the National Association of Manufacturers, the National Taxpayers Union, and the National Association of Realtors. Then came the Chamber of Commerce of the United States, the National Association of Wholesalers, Distributors and Affiliated Organizations, the American Bakers Association, Citizens for America, Citizens' Choice, and many others. More recently, the American Bankers Association, the National Association of Home Builders, and Citizens for a Sound Economy have joined the cause.

AMENDMENT WINS IN SENATE, SANDBAGGED IN HOUSE

In 1981, when Senator Orrin Hatch (R-UT) became Chairman and Senator Dennis DeConcini (D-AZ) became the ranking minority member of the Senate Judiciary Subcommittee on the Constitution, efforts began in earnest to develop an amendment that integrated the concepts of a balanced budget with a limitation on the growth of taxes and spending. After months of careful deliberation, the Tax Limitation/Balanced Budget Amendment was fashioned. It is that amendment which, in 1982, passed the United States Senate by a vote of 69 to 31.

The House of Representatives would not hear of it. House Speaker Thomas P. "Tip" O'Neill, Jr., (D-MA), Congressman Peter Rodino (D-NJ), Chairman of the House Judiciary Committee, and other House leaders had built their careers on taxing and spending. They feared that the amendment would end their spending binge; and they would not let it out of committee. A discharge petition was launched to force the measure to the House floor. After an intensive effort, the discharge was successful with only two days left in the session. Although we ran out of time to solidify our vote base, and were plagued by last-minute procedural sleight-of-hand by Tip O'Neill, the amendment garnered a substantial majority, but not the two-thirds necessary for a constitutional amendment.

ANOTHER SENATE VOTE—1986

In the 99th Congress, under the leadership of Majority Leader Bob Dole, debate and vote on a balanced budget amendment, Senate Joint Resolution 225, was scheduled in the U.S. Senate. Only a few months earlier Congress had passed (reluctantly) the Gramm-Rudman-Hollings Emergency Deficit Reduction Act (GRH). As consideration of the amendment unfolded, several of its opponents used GRH as their justification for voting against the amendment, claiming that "we ought to first see if a law will get the job done." Prime sponsor of GRH, Phil Gramm, a major supporter of the balanced budget amendment, said that the amendment was absolutely essential to make permanent any gains achieved under GRH.

The vote in the Senate came in March 1986. A bipartisan group of 66 Senators voted aye. Any one of the 34

Senators who voted nay could have put us over the top and forced the issue in the House.

AGONIZINGLY CLOSE

The two-thirds vote requirement for a constitutional amendment is a very tough one to meet. We have remained agonizingly close to our goal. During the 100th Congress, in the House of Representatives, a tax limitation/balanced budget amendment was introduced with more than half the members as co- sponsors (some 240). It takes 290 votes (if all are present) to pass an amendment in the House. That is an achievable number if proponents can force the measure to the floor for a straight up-or-down vote.

Former House Speaker Jim Wright, an arch enemy of the amendment, prevented it from coming to the floor for a vote, despite polls which reveal that 80 percent or more of the American people want an amendment. A repetition of our 1982 discharge petition effort is likely to be necessary to "blast" the amendment out of committee and on to the floor for a vote. The role of the states in the effort to achieve a balanced federal budget resolution, under Article V of the Constitution, is vital to achieving this political threshold.

CHAPTER 16

THE ROLE OF
THE STATES IN
PURSUIT OF
AN AMENDMENT

(Article V) . . . equally enables the general and the
state governments to originate the amendment of errors, as they may be pointed out by the experience on
the one side, or on the other.

(Federalist 43)

WHEN the Founding Fathers met in Philadelphia in 1787
to shape the United States Constitution, they determined
that one of the fundamental flaws of the Articles of Confederation was that it required a unanimous vote to amend
the Articles. Recognizing that the people would want to
change the Constitution from time to time, there was a
consensus that the amendment process should be difficult
but not impossible.

THE POWER TO AMEND

The debate at Philadelphia narrowed to the question: who
is to have the power to recommend and approve amend-

ments, the Congress or the states? On May 29, 1787, Edmund Randolph, Governor of Virginia, offered the Virginia proposal which excluded the "national legislature" entirely from the amendment process, leaving that authority to the states. George Mason explained, "It would be improper to require the consent of the national legislature, because they may abuse their power, and refuse their consent on that very account."[1]

When the Committee of Detail reported to the convention on August 6, its draft read: "On application of the legislatures of two-thirds of the states in the Union, for *an amendment* of this Constitution, the legislature of the United States shall call a convention for that purpose."[2] (Emphasis added.) This provision contemplated single amendments, the states alone triggered the process, the national legislature played no role except as an agent to convene the convention; and the convention method was selected as the means of not only developing the amendment but also of actually making it (ratifying it) a legally binding part of the Constitution.

STATES CO-EQUAL IN PROPOSING AMENDMENTS

On September 10, the convention debated the amendment provision. The Founders vacillated between a limited role for the Congress (the Virginia plan) and a limited role for the states, with no convention (the federalists' proposal). Finally, on September 15, George Mason repeated his concern that without a convention provision, the Congress might never propose "amendments of the proper kind"— those that might be inimical to its power. Amendment-proposing authority was affirmed for the Congress, and for the states through the convention process. The separate step of ratification became the sole province of the states, requiring approval by three-fourths of the states, irrespective of whether amendments were proposed by Congress or a state-convened convention.[3]

It is clear that the Founders, in devising the convention process for state-initiated amendments, considered it an important safeguard against, and a limit upon, an overbearing central government. They viewed the states as co-equal with the Congress in proposing amendments. The convention process was not "a last resort."

STATE ARTICLE V POWER DISCIPLINES CONGRESS

Although we've not had an Article V convention, the very fact that the procedure exists tends to keep Congress more honest and responsive. For example, early in this century—after years of resistance by the Senate to the direct election of Senators—states began to adopt resolutions calling on Congress to pass such an amendment or to convene a constitutional convention for the purpose of framing such an amendment. When the number of state resolutions was just one shy of the required two-thirds, the Senate finally capitulated, approved an amendment and sent it to the states for ratification. The Senators recognized that unless they designed that amendment themselves, a convention might not allow them to complete their terms but, rather, require each of them to stand for election immediately.

DRIVE FOR STATE RESOLUTIONS LAUNCHED

The first Article V state resolution for a balanced budget amendment was passed in 1975. State Senator Jim Clark in Maryland and State Representative David Halbrook in Mississippi started the drive with resolutions in their respective states.

In 1979, the balanced budget amendment had garnered 29 state resolutions (34 are needed). In 1979, Governor Jerry Brown of California publicly announced his support for the Article V resolution process and led an unsuccessful effort to persuade the liberal Ways and Means Committee of the California Assembly to approve the resolution.

Because Jerry Brown had thrown his hat in the ring for the Democratic presidential nomination, the resolution-gathering process became embroiled in presidential politics. Carter's White House formed a task force to oppose the resolution effort. Well coordinated opposition began to emerge.[4]

O'NEILL FEARED THE STATES

Nevertheless, New Hampshire passed a balanced budget amendment resolution in 1979 to become the 30th state. Speaker of the New Hampshire House of Representatives, George Roberts, travelled to Washington to present the resolution to House Speaker Tip O'Neill in person. Roberts challenged O'Neill to allow Congress to pass a balanced budget amendment. O'Neill demurred but said he would see to the passage of an amendment if a 33rd state submitted an Article V resolution to Congress.[5] Obviously, O'Neill did not want a citizen convention writing the taxing, spending, and deficit rules by which Congress would have to live. It is probably not a coincidence that Tip O'Neill's son, the Lieutenant Governor of Massachusetts, helped found an organization to combat the resolution drive.

LIBERAL COURTS BLOCK INITIATIVES

In 1982-83, respectively, the Alaska and Missouri legislatures passed resolutions. In 1983-84, initiative efforts were launched in California and Montana. The initiatives took a dual approach: a directive to the legislature to approve the resolution and send it on to Congress; and, concurrently, approval of a specific resolution by the voters (as a sort of "super-legislature") to be submitted to Congress if the legislature failed to comply with the initiatives' mandates.

The liberal Rose Bird-led California Supreme Court took an unprecedented step and ordered the measure off the ballot *before the people had a chance to vote on it.* The liberal Montana Supreme Court, emboldened by the California decision, took the same action. The people were denied an opportunity to address the issue themselves as a means of circumventing their recalcitrant legislatures.

LIBERAL "FRONT GROUP" OPPOSES
STATE RESOLUTIONS

The power and importance of the state resolution process for the balanced budget amendment became as clear to the enemies of federal fiscal discipline as it was to those of us seeking to pass an amendment. In 1983, the AFL-CIO, and other foes of the amendment, formed a committee that they disingenuously called "Citizens to Protect the Constitution." Among those joining the AFL-CIO in their enterprise were (partial list): American Association of University Professors; American Association of University Women; American Civil Liberties Union; American Federation of Teachers; Americans for Democratic Action; American Jewish Congress; Americans for Indian Opportunity; Americans for Religious Liberty; American Federation of State, County and Municipal Employees; B'nai B'rith International; Center for Community Change; Communications Workers of America; Consumer Federation of America; General Board of Church and Society, United Methodist Church; International Association of Machinists and Aerospace Workers; International Ladies Garment Workers Union; International Union of Electrical Workers; Leadership Conference on Civil Rights; National Association for the Advancement of Colored People; National Association of Letter Carriers; National Bar Association; National Council of La Raza; National Council of Senior Citizens; National Education Association; National Farmers Union; National Legal Aid & Defender Association; National Organization for Women; National Urban League; National Women's Political Caucus; People for the American Way; Service Employees International Union; United Auto Workers; United Mine Workers; United Steel Workers of America.

(While the list appears to be top heavy with labor unions, this is an anomaly. Private sector union *members* support a balanced budget amendment as vigorously as do non-union workers. It is labor *leaders,* especially those in charge of unions comprised of government workers, who oppose constitutional constraints on government purse strings.)

"RUNAWAY CONVENTION"—LIBERALS' RED HERRING

These organizations had found that "stonewalling" state constitutional convention resolutions by challenging the *substance* of the tax limitation/balanced budget amendment was not working. Nationwide, Americans overwhelmingly supported such an amendment. Hence, our opponents shifted their strategy and began generating fears of the constitutional convention *process*. They fashioned the specter of a convention running amok—a so-called "runaway" convention—repealing the Bill of Rights and dismantling the constitutional framework.

You can imagine the frustration of those of us seeking Article V state resolutions when, during the legislative hearings in Michigan in 1984, we heard representatives of the ACLU, public employees unions, welfare rights groups, etc., talk about our beautiful, pristine Constitution, claiming that we dare not risk changing one word or one concept in this precious document, and that a citizen convention was an unacceptable risk. These are the very same individuals and groups who, for more than half a century, have done everything possible to rewrite the Constitution, through court decisions and congressional action, in order to concentrate power in Washington and subvert the power of states, local governments, private organizations, and individuals. Having been successful in dismantling the restraints against federal intervention in state-local-private matters through redefinition of the Commerce Clause, the General Welfare Clause, and so forth, these selfsame guardians of the public weal claim we cannot risk any changes in the sacred document, especially at the hands of *the people*.

SOME CONSERVATIVES TAKE THE BAIT

Such unabashed duplicity on the part of liberals was not entirely unexpected. What we did not anticipate was that some conservatives, even some experienced in the political process, would become handmaidens to the liberals in trying to block the state resolution process. These include the Liberty Lobby, an overtly anti-Semitic group, the John Birch Society, Eagle Forum, and a handful of others who find themselves in league with the liberal organizations listed above.

"BLIZZARD" OF OBJECTIONS UNFOUNDED

Opponents of the Article V convention process assert the same shopworn claims and falsehoods from state to state, counting on the "blizzard" of objections to stimulate apoplexy among unwitting citizens who may have been exposed to the Article V issue for the first time. In turn, concerned constituents harass and seek to intimidate legislators with cajolery and threats. It is political mob psychology at its worst.

Article V was placed in the Constitution by the Founders as the people's safeguard against a tyrannical Congress. The arguments of contemporary opponents of Article V are unsupported by constitutional history, legal precedent, or common sense. In the Postscript to this chapter we have set forth claims of both the left and the right in opposition to the use of Article V resolutions—and our responses to them. I urge you to consider them carefully.

STATE POWER TO DISCIPLINE WASHINGTON JEOPARDIZED

The grave risk inherent in the conduct of our opponents is that if they are successful in thwarting use of thc convention-resolution process vis-à-vis the balanced budget amendment, the states' authority and power to initiate amendments on any subject will be dealt a mortal blow. Other much needed reforms of and limitations upon federal excesses, which the Congress itself would never propose, will be lost to us forever. Those are the stakes.

Another dimension of this battle, as John Noonan, a former constitutional law professor and now a federal judge, has pointed out, has to do with popular discipline of the federal courts. The Supreme Court has rendered decisions that constitute amendments to the U.S. Constitution, such as the 1962 decision on school prayer that essentially amended the Constitution to read, "No prayer shall be offered in a public school," and the 1973 decision on abortion that as an amendment would have read: "Abortion shall be the right of every pregnant woman." In so doing the Court has exercised both the proposing and ratifying powers without regard to the requirements of Article V.

If we forever abandon the people's convention-calling authority, we will not only forfeit the right to *initiate* amendments restraining the federal government, we will relinquish the power to revoke "amendments" imposed on us by court decisions (wherein the people's right to "ratification" is non-existent). It is no wonder liberals are clamoring to preside over the funeral of Article V's state resolution power. That power is the ultimate sword of Damocles over the left's agenda.

POSTSCRIPT 1

CLAIMS AND RESPONSES REGARDING THE ARTICLE V CONVENTION PROCESS

Liberal and conservative opponents make the following claims:

Claim—The Founders never intended, and Article V does not provide for, limiting state-called conventions to a single subject. States can make application only for an "open" convention which could address any and all provisions of the Constitution.

Response—In his recent book, "Constitutional Brinksmanship: Amending the Constitution by National Convention," an exhaustive study of all aspects of the convention issue, Russell L. Caplan says:

> Article V does not expressly say that an application must specify a particular subject area or proposed text for an amendment, and Charles Black has argued that article V authorizes only a plenary assembly, hence that petitions for a limited convention are invalid. That rule would disqualify nearly all the balanced-budget applications, which purport to limit the convention to that topic or even the exact text of the amendment set out in the application. To judge, however, from evidence of the founding era, Black's position is erroneous. . . . Despite the nebulous quality of article V's phrase "a Convention for proposing Amendments," applications must evidently specify particular amendments, and a convention need be called only if the requisite number of applications agree in text or subject matter with regard to at least one amendment. The phrase 'for proposing Amendments' refers to the purpose or type of convention intended, in this case, as Madison referred to it at Philadelphia, "a Convention for the purpose of amendments"—in contrast to, for example, the trade conventions of the 1770s held to propose state statutes. The phrase does not, as Charles Black and others have held, preclude limitation to a single subject.
>
> Contrary to what John Calhoun and Professor Black supposed, therefore, a convention is not to be used only for thoroughgoing

revision of the Constitution. _Each_ amendment under article V, said Hamilton in The Federalist, _whether from Congress or a convention_ "would be a _single proposition_, and might be brought forward _singly_." One of Madison's points in his Report on the Virginia Resolutions was that a convention could be called for _one well-defined purpose_, a position unchanged in his 1830 North American Review essay ("two thirds of the States to institute and three fourths to effectuate _an amendment_") and echoed the following year by the Supreme Court in Smith v. Union Bank of George-town. . . . "Cassius," the federalist Boston merchant James Sullivan, wrote: "The 5th article also provides, that the states may propose any alterations which they see fit, and that Congress shall take measures for having them carried into effect." Should the new Constitution be ratified, said Hamilton in Federalist 85, "alterations in it may at any time be effected by nine states," nine states being then _two_ thirds. "And consequently whenever nine or rather ten states, were united in the desire of _a particular amendment_, that amendment must infallibly take place," Hamilton adding that "though two-thirds may set on foot _the measure_, three-fourths must ratify." It seems impossible for two thirds of the states to initiate or effect "a particular amendment" unless a particular subject is specified in each application, and unless the applications agree on the subject."6 (Emphasis added.)

Some years after the convention, Madison, in his 1799 Report on the Virginia Resolutions, said that the states might apply for a convention to address exclusively the alien and sedition acts:

The Legislatures of the States have a right also to originate amendments to the Constitution, by a concurrence of two- thirds of the whole number, in applications to Congress for the purpose. Accordingly, the state legislatures might obtain repeal of the Alien and Sedition Acts by requesting Congress to 'propose an explanatory amendment to the Constitution' declaring the rights such acts violated; or two-thirds of themselves, if such had been their option, might, by an application to Congress, have obtained a Convention for _the same object_.7 (Emphasis added.)

The blue-ribbon ABA committee which studied this question exhaustively in 1974 reported:

> We are led to conclude that there is no justification for the view that Article V sanctions only general conventions. Such an interpretation would relegate the alternative method to an 'unequal' method of initiating amendments.. Even if the state legislatures overwhelmingly felt that there was a necessity for limited change in the Constitution, they would be discouraged from calling for a convention if that convention would automatically have the power to propose a complete revision of the Constitution.
>
> Since Article V specifically and exclusively vests the state legislatures with the authority to apply for a convention, we can perceive no sound reason as to why they cannot invoke limitations in exercising that authority.[8]

In September 1987, the U.S. Dept. of Justice released its careful analysis of the limited constitutional convention issue, concluding

> . . . that Article V does permit a limited convention. This conclusion is premised on three arguments. First, Article V provides for an equality of the Congress and the states in the power to initiate constitutional change. Since the Congress may limit its attention to single issues . . . the states also have [the same] . . . Second, consensus about the need for constitutional change is a prerequisite . . . [This] requirement is better met by the view that Article V permits limited constitutional conventions . . . Third, history and the practice of both the states and the Congress show a common understanding that the Constitution can be amended issue by issue, regardless of the method by which the amendment process is initiated."[9] (Emphasis added.)

If the words of the Founders and the results of these authoritative, exhaustive studies are not enough, common sense and actual practices of the Congress with respect to state convention-call applications should dispatch the issue. Over the years Congress has received hundreds of state applications, all of which have focused on specific subjects: direct election of Senators, school prayer, the "one man, one vote" decision, the balanced budget amendment, etc. At any one time well more than the requisite two-thirds of the states may have one or more applications pending before the Congress, albeit on different subjects. Right now there are such applications from 39 separate states.

If, as opponents of the process claim, Congress may convene only a <u>general</u> convention (which must mean that Congress is to ignore the subject matter set forth in each application), well more than the 34 applications necessary to trigger a convention have been presented. Why then is there not a resolution for a general convention now pending before the Congress? Simply because everyone understands that subject matter consensus is relevant—and as yet there are not 34 resolutions on the same subject—and when there are, Congress will be obliged to get at the business of calling a convention on <u>that</u> subject.

It makes absolutely no sense to say that Congress is awaiting 34 state applications on a <u>particular subject</u> which, when received, will obligate it to convene a convention with <u>plenary</u> powers. No—compatibility of subject matter is important precisely because Congress, which wants no amendments it does not originate, is not about to give any greater scope than it must to a convention it doesn't want in the first place.

<u>Claim</u>—Even if Congress seeks to limit an Article V convention to a single subject, it cannot control the convention once it is launched. The convention would be sovereign and could do anything it wished. The convention can and will "run away," repealing the Bill of Rights and other key protections of the Constitution and proposing all kinds of new amendments. It will wreck the Constitution.

<u>Response</u>—One is first struck by the opinion of their fellow citizens held by opponents of the Article V convention process: citizen delegates, selected for their position (whatever that might be) on the balanced budget amendment issue, would go into a type of "feeding frenzy" upon arrival at a convention; they would ignore the subject matter mandate and tear at the entrails of

American constitutional government. Where is the evidence the people don't like our Bill of Rights or the basic framework of our government? Polls reveal they don't like large deficits and federal fiscal malfeasance. It is logical they would devote themselves to that topic as assigned by the convening authority.

The notion of delegates acting obscenely would have been alien to the Founders: "Nothing would surprise the framers more than the confusion surrounding the convention method of amendment, for it was common and accepted in their time. The convention route had been built with familiar materials; it was not intended to be, nor did it start out as, an especially clandestine procedure." [10]

As to legal restraints on the power of an Article V convention, the ABA study concluded: "There is the view, with which we disagree, that an Article V convention would be a sovereign assemblage and could not be restricted by either the state legislatures or the Congress in its authority or proposals. And there is the view, with which we agree, that Congress has the power to establish procedures which would limit a convention's authority to a specific subject matter where the legislatures of two-thirds of the states seek a convention limited to that subject. [11]

Other leading bipartisan constitutional authorities, legal analysts and scholars share this view:

• *The late U.S. Senator Sam Ervin, constitutional law scholar—*

This construction [that a convention cannot be limited] would effectively destroy the power of the States to originate the amendment of errors pointed out by experience, as Madison expected them to do. Alternatively, under that construction, applications for a limited convention deriving in some States with a dissatisfaction with the school desegregation cases, in others because of the school prayer cases, and in still others by reason of objection to the <u>Miranda</u> rule, could all be combined to make up the requisite two-thirds of the States needed to meet the requirements of Article V. [12]

• *Griffin Bell, Attorney General of the United States under President Jimmy Carter—*

> *Today's congressmen, especially those who resist the idea of a balanced budget amendment in the first place . . . resist the idea (of an Article V convention) in the strongest possible terms. They warn of a "runaway convention." Never mind that, as a matter of law and common sense, this is nonsense.*
>
> *Suppose Congress does what I don't expect it to do, and summons a constitutional convention rather than draft an amendment itself. Congress would give that convention a very narrow mandate, just as the state legislatures have done. By law, the delegates would be limited to drafting this one amendment, and nothing else. If they somehow draft something about abortion, or some other extraneous issue, Congress could refuse to submit it to the states for ratification; just 13 or more of the 50 states could refuse to ratify it, thereby defeating it; or the U.S. Supreme Court could invalidate the delegates' actions as violation of their limited constitutional mandate.*
>
> *So a "runaway convention" is flatly impossible. But what is possible is what economists call a "runaway debt." It's a terrifying prospect."* [13]

• *John Noonan—*

> *If the States apply for a convention on a balanced budget, Congress must call a convention on a balanced budget. It cannot at its pleasure enlarge the topics. Nor can the convention go beyond what Congress has specified in the call. The convention's powers are derived from Article V and they cannot exceed what Article V specifies. The convention meets at the call of Congress on the subject which the States have set out and Congress has called the convention for.* [14]

• *William W. Van Alstyne, Professor of Law, Duke University—*

It is perfectly remarkable that some have argued for a construction [of Article V] not merely limiting the power of State legislatures to have a convention, but limiting that power to its least expected, least appropriate, most difficult (and yet most dangerous) use. [15]

• *Professor Aaron Wildavsky, Political Science Dept., Graduate School of Public Policy, University of California, Berkeley—*

Suppose you, the reader, or I, or anyone, were given the task of managing a convention that instead of dealing with budget balance and spending limits would fundamentally alter the Constitution in such a way that three-quarters of the states would approve. Immediately the immensity of the task and the sheer unlikelihood of its accomplishment would come crashing down on us. No one would bet a dollar on its behalf. (Those who wish to contribute to my income should write proposing wagers.) [16]

• *Professor Henry Campbell Black—*

A constitutional convention has no authority to enact legislation of a general sort, and if the convention is called for the purpose of amending the Constitution in a specific part, the delegates have no power to act upon and propose amendments in other parts of the Constitution. [17]

• *Professor Paul J. Weber, Dept. of Political Science, University of Louisville—*

Amending the federal constitution by means of a constitutional convention would be one of the safest political procedures the nation could pursue. The political constraints insure that no convention can get out of control.

There are at least six such constraints: the character of the delegates elected; the public campaign statements and promises of the delegates; the number of delegates and divisions within the convention itself which would make it extraordinarily difficult for one faction or a radical position to prevail; the constant awareness that whatever the convention proposes must be presented to Congress; the Supreme Court which, upon appeal, might well declare certain actions beyond the constitutional powers of the convention; and most important of all, [ratification] by 38 states. One could hardly imagine more effective constraints on a constitutional convention.[18]

The following are claims advanced by opponents on the right.

Claim—That the Constitution is perfect and divinely inspired. We cannot risk any changes to the Constitution and, therefore, must not utilize the convention method.

Response—The key thing to remember is that the convention triggering power of the states is an integral part of the Constitution, placed there by the Founders in their wisdom for just such a circumstance as we face today. As John Noonan has said,

> Respect, indeed reverence, for the Constitution is a proper attitude for conservatives to cultivate. Is it respectful to the Constitution to maintain that of the two methods of amendment specified in Article V, one is too dangerous to be put to use? True respect for the Constitution calls conservatives to see the wisdom of the Founders in assuring that the states can act when the self interest of Congress prevents its acting to correct errors; that the states can focus a convention on a single amendment; and that we have the same or greater assurances against unwarranted, outrageous innovations by a convention than we possess against subversion of the Constitution by Congress.
>
> Overwhelming majorities in nearly every state have indicated support for the requirements of a balanced federal budget. Few dare oppose it on its merits. Its friends should not hesitate to achieve it by a convention that will be narrowly focused, profoundly democratic, and eminently constitutional.[19]

Claim—That liberals have hatched a plot, a conspiracy, if you will, to make radical changes in the Constitution. In their arti-

cles, "Plotting to Rewrite the U.S. Constitution," and "Bicentennial Plot," Phyllis Schlafly (Eagle Forum) and Gary Benoit (Birch Society), respectively, focus on a Washington-based discussion group called the "Committee on the Constitutional System" (CCS). They claim CCS is waiting for an Article V convention, called for balanced budget amendment purposes. They intend to seize control of the convention, and through it install a parliamentary-type government on America.[20]

Response—CCS is a discussion and study group which numbers among its participants Attorney General Richard Thornburgh. CCS's published papers—"Reforming American Government—the Bicentennial Papers of the Constitutional System"—contain an essay entitled "Why Risk a Constitutional Convention."[21] The essay is a clear statement of opposition to a convention. Apparently the very organization accused of leading the conspiracy for a convention doesn't want a convention.

C. Herman Pritchett, a political scientist from U.C. Santa Barbara, who wrote the referenced essay, stated, "Calling a convention for budget balancing or any other purpose is playing <u>Russian roulette</u> with the Constitution."[22] This is precisely the phrase which Phyllis Schlafly has seized upon and has used as the lead line in her report, "Combatting Chicanery about the Constitution." Her repetition of this phrase, utilized by Pritchett, who makes it clear he doesn't want a balanced budget amendment to the Constitution in any event, has prompted her followers to propagate the fear naturally associated with placing a revolver to one's head. John Noonan notes that:

> *Conservative critics have feared that the liberal elite could manipulate a convention more easily than it can Congress. Is this fear plausible?" asks John Noonan. "Congress is currently elected from many districts gerrymandered by predominantly Democratic legislatures. If the convention delegates are elected on the basis other than congressional districts, they will represent more accurately the majority that elected Ronald Reagan. If the delegates are elected from congressional districts, they will not be worse than the incumbents, and maybe better.*

Incumbents running for office are favored by their incumbency; the Democrats in the House have benefitted from this factor. Elections for convention delegates would be an open contest. There will be no incumbents. Moreover, the election of congressmen involves many tradeoffs in the minds of the voters. Stands on particular issues are often discounted. In an election for delegates to a convention to act on the balanced budget, the issue will be single and simple: is the candidate for or against the balanced budget amendment? A clearer choice will predictably lead to the election of delegates less open to manipulation, less dependent upon the whole webs of special interests.[23]

In the last few years, in several states we have been within a handful of votes of securing our 33rd and 34th states. If there were a national conspiracy among liberals seeking a constitutional convention so that they might subvert the Constitution, surely they could have influenced four or five liberal state representatives and senators to vote with us so that a convention could be assured. That did not happen. There wasn't any indication whatever that _any_ liberal or group of liberals aided our cause. My only conclusion is that those on the right worried about a liberal conspiracy will have to organize it, because to date it has not materialized.

Claim—That Ronald Reagan opposes the convention method of amending the U.S. Constitution and is fearful of it.

Response—This has been a crucial misrepresentation because of the respect which most conservatives have for Mr. Reagan and, of course, because of the power and leadership naturally flowing from the Office of the President. In a letter dated February 23, 1987, to Eagle Forum members in Montana, at the time of consideration by the Montana Legislature of the convention call resolution, Phyllis Schlafly said "He (Ronald Reagan) supports a balanced budget amendment, but he does not support a constitutional convention. The 'Public Papers of the Presidents' quote Ronald Reagan as as (sic) answering a question about a constitutional convention by saying, 'Once it's open, they could *take up any number of things."' In fact, on March 26, 1986, the year prior, the White House issued a statement to reporters immediately following the defeat of the balanced budget amendment in the U.S. Senate (by a single vote): "It remains the President's hope that Congress will act responsibly to pass a balanced budget amendment, avoiding the need for a constitutional convention . . . The President urges Congress to set aside its free-spending habits and to promptly act to propose a balanced budget amendment before the supporters of such an amendment have no other course than to pursue petitioning the remaining state legislatures."*

A few days after the Schlafly Montana letter, Ronald Reagan signed the following letter to the Minority Leader of the Montana State Senate:

> *I am pleased to respond to your request for my views on the resolution now before the Montana Legislature, petitioning Congress to call for a constitutional convention for the purpose of drafting an amendment that would require a balanced Federal budget.*
>
> *I have long supported an amendment to the Constitution that would require the Federal budget to be balanced. I have championed that cause in Congress on several occasions, calling on the public and State officials and legislators to make their views known. Thus far, all of these efforts have not been successful in persuading Congress, although last year such an amendment failed to gain the necessary two-thirds affirmative vote in the Senate by the slimmest margin of one vote. It has now become obvious that without further State initiatives Congress will not act to impose a limit on its own spending.*
>
> *I therefore believe that further action by the States, and particularly by the Montana Legislature, in petitioning Congress to call for a constitutional convention for the sole purpose of writing a balanced budget amendment will go far towards convincing Congress to pass and submit to the States an amendment for this purpose. If your effort is successful, Montana would be the 33rd State to pass such a resolution, just one short of the 34 required to call a constitutional convention. I believe this may finally convince*

Congress to act on an amendment of its own, which has always been my goal.

I hope these views will be helpful to you as you continue your deliberations.

<u>*Claim*</u>—*That an Article V convention could and would change the method of ratification to assure approval of its radical amendments (thereby eliminating the existing constitutional safeguard of ratification by three-quarters (38) of the states.)*

<u>*Response*</u>—*Because it is so obvious that the ratification hurdle would pre-empt any bizarre and wholesale mutilation of the Constitution, opponents have been obliged to conjure up a scenario in which convention delegates would subvert the current ratification process. Presumably the convention would circumvent Congress and send its work product directly to the states with instructions to ratify under some new set of rules.*

On its face, this claim should self destruct. But beyond that we have the benefit of the wisdom of the father of the Constitution, James Madison, on this point. He said, "My idea of the sovereignty of the people is, that the people can change the Constitution if they please; but while the Constitution exists, they must conform themselves to its dictates." As Russell Caplan notes:

. . . An Article V convention proposing <u>ultra vires</u> amendments still professes to act within the Constitution. The standards of the Confederation were discarded at Philadelphia, but the standards of the Constitution must govern any non-plenary Article V convention. In the words of a state court, 'the Constitution may be set aside by revolution, but it can only be amended in the way it provides.' . . . For its part, if <u>a convention should try to force an amendment through the states without obtaining a congressional decision on the mode of ratification, the amendment—whether within the convention's mandate or not—would remain invalid.</u> Likewise invalid would be an amendment requiring no ratification, or ratification by a reduced number of states. If a convention submitted a measure purporting to be legislation binding without passage by Congress, Congress would be able to obtain an injunction to prevent enforcement, since it could allege injury to its law-

making powers. At the first session of the 1790 Rhode Island ratifying convention, delegate Henry Marchant, later a federal judge, said: 'If we look into the Act by which we met, we shall find why & how we met here. We have no Legislative Power. Have no other Powers than as trustees for the business.'[24] *(Emphasis added.)*

Our final category is those claims asserted by opponents of the Article V convention who control the Congress.

Claim—That an Article V convention would launch the Nation into uncharted waters in terms of rules and procedures about which the Constitution is silent. There are many open questions, there are few answers; an Article V convention is risky business.

Response—Just as it has served Congress's interest to maintain that a convention cannot be limited, thereby dissuading states from submitting applications and leaving Congress in exclusive control of the amendment process, Congress promotes other uncertainties, as well. ". . . Congress, especially the liberal establishment concentrated for the last 30 years in the House of Representatives, has an interest in leaving the (convention) route undefined," explains Russell Caplan. "Don Edwards, Chair of a House Judiciary subcommittee, finds 'no assurance' that a national convention 'could not be a runaway,' and opposes a procedures bill on the ground it would aid the drive for a convention: 'Anything that encourages this sort of utilization of Article V is unwise.' The more obscure the process, the easier it is for Congress to discourage pressure by rejecting applications on technical grounds—a phenomenon that has been aptly called the "politics of uncertainty."

For this reason, Congress has never established a procedure for receiving and verifying applications, never promulgated guidelines for applications or for the convention itself. Congress could have done so long ago, Justice Scalia has said, by amending Article V if necessary. "But the Congress is not about to do that. It likes the existing confusion, because that deters resort to *the convention process. <u>It does not want amending power to be anywhere but in its own hands</u>. . . .*[25] *(Emphasis added.)*

Conclusion. Cutting through all of the hysteria which opponents of the Article V convention process intentionally or unwittingly have generated is this simple conclusion by the scholar who has most recently and exhaustively reviewed the issue: "The evidence indicates that both plenary and limited topic conventions may be applied for, and that a limited convention is bound by Article V to propose only those amendments described in the triggering applications. Amendments proposed by a limited convention on topics not specified may be withheld by Congress from ratification and additionally can, for the most part, be challenged in the federal courts."[26] *(Emphasis added.)*

CHAPTER 17

WHERE DO WE GO FROM HERE?

> On the plains of hesitation bleach the bones of countless millions who, at the dawn of victory, sat down to rest and, resting, died.
>
> (*Unknown poet*)

THE political pundits say we are at a crossroads. We are about to choose a new vision for America. It may be the route charted by Ronald Reagan and George Bush, or we may head off in some other direction, presumably increasing the size and power of government.

But there is no doubt about the direction in which our nation is headed on the issue of the tax limitation/balanced budget amendment. There is virtual unanimity that it is immoral to pass our deficits on to our children and grandchildren. The years of effort have laid the foundation for the success of our amendment. The next steps are a matter of timing and strategy. We must keep fighting on Capitol Hill and in the states to push the amendment over the top.

With President Bush committed to the amendment, and willing to devote some political "capital" to the battle, our congressional vanguard should be reinvigorated.

207

CALL TO ARMS FOR STATE LEADERS

In the states, it is time the governors united behind our state resolution effort in order to preserve the amendment-initiating power for the states collectively. It is their bulwark against "runaway" Washington. They ought to be outraged at members of Congress who behind the scenes threaten state legislators with loss of federal funds if they vote to exercise their Article V amendment powers.

It is also about time that state legislators immersed themselves in, and became students of, the history of the Philadelphia convention that gave them amendatory powers. They must come to appreciate *why* the Founders gave such powers to the states. Then they will be less likely to be intimidated by convention-call opponents, whether of the left or right.

DE TOCQUEVILLE'S VISIONS OF AMERICA

Alexis de Tocqueville, in *Democracy in America*, described early 19th century America as a sharing, caring society in which community needs were met by the voluntary association of private citizens. We were—and still are—driven by a charitable impulse. Our great hospitals, universities, foundations, and service, civic, and fraternal organizations have been privately created.

De Tocqueville, contrasting the American experience with the European, noted that problem-solving in France was the province of the bureaucracy and in England the burden of the upper class. In America, the people were wary of bureaucratic intervention, intolerant of class distinctions, and were especially sensitive to taxation about which—at least in part—they had recently fought a war. America was still heavily influenced by biblical perspectives on taxes: "If he [the sinner] refuses to listen even to the church, treat him as you would a pagan *or a tax collector.*" (Matthew 18:17) (Emphasis added.) To the early Christians, the tax collector represented the long arm of the Roman Empire, collecting a tribute to support an alien culture that kept the taxpayer in subjugation. To the colonists it was the British Empire; to today's American citizen it is the Empire of Washington.

AMERICA'S GOODNESS

Voluntarily solving problems is the most cost-effective, humane, personally satisfying approach. The structures of volunteerism are already in place—our churches, civic organizations, service clubs, and fraternal orders. Government—especially the federal government—has been trying to "crowd us out." de Tocqueville discerned that America is great because America is good. But he warned that if she ceased to be good, she would cease to be great. *Voluntary* interdependence will assure that goodness and greatness.

WE CAN CONTROL OUR DESTINY

The tax limitation/balanced budget amendment is the linchpin of a new era of political discipline. Its passage will demonstrate that *we the people* can control our destiny, that national bankruptcy is not inevitable. We will create a renewed vitality in representative government. Once again our actions will be a beacon to the rest of the world, giving others confidence that they can lick their own government spending/deficit monster as well.

God forbid that we should rest on the "plains of hesitation."

ENDNOTES

CHAPTER 1

1. Adam Smith, *An Inquiry Into the Nature and Causes of the Wealth of Nations* (1776), Book Four, chapter 7, "Of Colonies," part 2.
2. "Facts and Figures on Government Finance" (Washington, DC: Tax Foundation, Inc., 1986), p. C32.
3. Ibid., p. B36.
4. "Budget of the United States Government, 1990," pp. 10-37.
5. Ibid.
6. William B. Irvine, "'Brutus': Anti-Federalist Hero," *The Wall Street Journal*, February 6, 1987, editorial page.

CHAPTER 2

1. Richard W. Rahn, "Treasury Report Vindicates 1981 Tax Cut," *Policy Working Papers of the United States Chamber of Commerce, #16* (May 1988), p. 3. It is estimated that in 1986 the top one percent of income taxpayers paid over 26 percent of total federal individual income tax payments.
2. Fiscal year 1989 estimated revenue from federal personal income tax is $425 billion and from social security is $244 billion. "Budget of the United States Government, 1990," pp. 10-28.

CHAPTER 3

1. Irvine, op. cit.
2. "Budget of the United States Government, 1989," pp. 5-159.

3. "Budget of the United States Government, 1990," pp. 10-38.

4. Ibid.

CHAPTER 4

1. Thomas Jefferson, letters to Governor Plumer, July 21, 1816, and to Samuel Kerchival, July 12, 1816, respectively; John P. Foley, ed., *The Jeffersonian Cyclopedia* (New York: Russell & Russell, 1967), vol. 1, p. 234; H.A. Washington, *The Writings of Thomas Jefferson* (New York: H.W. Derby, 1861), vol. VII, p. 41.

2. See the New York Times/CBS News Poll, "Constitution Poll" (May 11-14, 1987), p. 14. (A representative cross-section of the American population was surveyed on a number of issues, including the following question: Would you favor or oppose a constitutional amendment requiring the federal government to balance its budget? The response was: favor 85%, oppose 10%, don't know/no answer 6%. The report indicates that the support for a constitutional balanced budget amendment has increased over the last decade.

3. News release from the Internal Revenue Service, Washington, DC, (January 4, 1989), p. 2

CHAPTER 5

1. "Facts and Figures on Government Finance," op. cit.; "Budget of the United States Government, 1989," pp. 6g-14 and pp. 6g-45; "Statistical Abstract of the United States (Washington, DC: US Department of Commerce, Bureau of the Census, 1986), p. 325.

2. "Budget of the United States Government, 1989," pp. 6g-45.

3. George B. Galloway, *History of the United States House of Representatives* (Washington, DC: US Government Printing Office, 1962), p. 110.

4. Ibid.; "Guide to Congress" (Washington, DC: *Congressional Quarterly,* Second Edition, 1976), p. 460.

5. Norman J. Ornstein, and others, "Vital Statistics on Congress" (Washington, DC: American Enterprise Institute, 1984-85 edition), *Studies in Political and Social Processes,* pp. 121–22, 124.

6. "Budget of the United States Government, 1990," pp. 9-12.

7. "Curbing the Frank," *The Wall Street Journal,* October 17, 1988, editorial page.

8. "Statistical Abstract of the United States," op. cit.

9. Mark Brisnow, "Congress: An Insider's Look at the Mess on Capitol Hill," *Newsweek,* January 4, 1988, p. 24.

10. Galloway, op. cit., p. 113.

CHAPTER 6

1. "Budget of the United States Government, 1990," pp. 5-135.

2. Craig Colgate, Jr., and others, *National Trade and Professional Associations of the United States,* (New York: Columbia Books, Inc., 1986, 21st Annual Edition), p. 16; Mary Jordan, "Trade Groups Flock to Region," *The Washington Post,* February 19, 1987, p. C1.

3. Jordan, op. cit., p. C10.

4. Jack Anderson, "Paying to be Plucked," *The Sacramento Bee,* December 23, 1974, p. B7.

5. Marshall J. Breger, "Halting Taxpayer Subsidy of Partisan Advocacy," (Washington, DC: The Heritage Foundation, 1983), *The Heritage Lectures #26;* James T. Bennett and Thomas J. DiLorenzo, "Destroying Democracy: How Government Funds Partisan Politics," (Washington, DC: Cato Institute, 1985).

6. Irvine, op. cit.

7. *The Wall Street Journal,* November 26, 1986, p. 20.

8. Robert L. Corn, "Campaign 'Reform': Monopolizing the Political Process" (Washington, DC: November/December 1987), *Policy Report,* p. 11.

9. Brooks Jackson, "Texas Candidates, Like Other House Challengers, Must Overcome Incumbent's Hefty Purse," *The Wall Street Journal,* September 24, 1986, p. 60; "Good- Time Charlies," *The Wall Street Journal,* August 8, 1988, editorial page.

10. Joe Scott, "The Political Animal" (May 4, 1987), Vol. 15, #9, p. 3.

CHAPTER 7

1. Mitzi Ayala, "Farm Subsidies Yield Costly Harvest," *The Wall Street Journal,* June 4, 1987, editorial page.

2. *The Chicago Tribune,* September 9, 1987, editorial page.

3. Gary Putka, "Troubling Statistics on Student-Loan Defaults Yield No Agreement on Explanation or Solution," *The Wall Street Journal,* March 15, 1988, p. 72; *The Sacramento Union,* November 7, 1988, p. 7.

4. John Johnson, "School Lunch Program Feeds Heavy Lobbying," *The Sacramento Bee,* May 13, 1985, p. A1.

5. Tim Carrington, "Air Force Renews Campaign to Scrap Fairchild Industries' T-46 Trainer Jet," *The Wall Street Journal,* December 10, 1986.

6. Edward H. Crane, "On the Problem of America's Policy Myopia" (Washington, DC: Cato Institute, January 1, 1987), *Vital Speeches of the Day,* p. 185.

7. "Goodbye, Washington," *The Wall Street Journal,* December 10, 1987, editorial page.

CHAPTER 8

1. "Hooray, A Drought!" *The Wall Street Journal,* August 4, 1988, p. 16.

2. Ibid.

3. Robert E. Taylor, "Conferees Clear $18 Billion Bill for Sewer Plants," *The Wall Street Journal,* October 13, 1986.

4. Daniel J. Mitchell, "The $6 Billion Overdose" (Washington, DC: Citizens for a Sound Economy, September 30, 1986), *Capitol Comment #20.*

5. Milton R. Copulos, "Why the Superfund Pork Barrel Deserves a Veto" (Washington, DC: The Heritage Foundation, October 9, 1986), *Executive Memorandum #136.*

6. "It Was a Joke (On You!): Federal Program Produced 35,000 Jobs—At a Cost of $88,751 Apiece," *The Sacramento Union,* January 31, 1987.

7. Bill Whalen, "Emergency Pork," *Insight Magazine,* June 8, 1987, p. 25.

8. Peter H. Rossi, "No Good Applied Social Research Goes Unpunished," *Applied Social Research Magazine,* November/December 1987, pp. 74-79.

9. Ibid., p. 77.

10. Martin Morse Wooster, "The Homeless Issue: An Adman's Dream," *Reason Magazine,* July 1987, p. 20.

11. Ibid., p. 27; Patrick Buchanan, "Mitch Snyder, Moral Bully," *The Sacramento Union,* January 8, 1989, p. 23.

12. Victor Geminian, "Assisting the Homeless: Grants or a 'Poorhouse'?" *The Sacramento Bee,* December 13, 1988, Opinion section. (The author is the executive director of Legal Services of Northern California.)

13. Wooster, op. cit., p. 27.

14. Ibid., p. 26.

15. J. P. Vettraino, "The Desperate Lives of the Kings of the Road," *The Sacramento Union,* October 9, 1988, p. 3.

16. David Whitman, "Who's Who Among the Homeless," *The New Republic,* February 8, 1988.

17. Charles Krauthammer, "How to Save the Homeless Mentally Ill," *The New Republic,* February 8, 1988, p. 24.

18. Charles Krauthammer, "Homeless Mentally Ill Must Be Removed From the Streets," *The Sacramento Union,* December 25, 1988, Opinion section.

19. Edgar O. Olsen, "Housing Subsidies Rise for the Needy," *The Wall Street Journal,* December 12, 1988, editorial page.

20. Vettraino, op. cit., p. 21.

CHAPTER 9

1. Charles Wolf, Jr., *Markets or Government: Choosing Between Imperfect Alternatives,* (Cambridge, MA: MIT Press, 1988); Keith Marsden, "Links Between Taxes and Economic Growth: Some Empirical Evidence," *World Bank Staff Working Paper #605,* Washington, DC, 1983.

2. Wolf, op. cit., p. 146.

3. Ibid., p. 141.

4. William A. Cox, "Wage Stagnation May Be Ending," *The Wall Street Journal*, August 29, 1988, p. 10.

5. *Economic Outlook*, Chamber of Commerce of the United States, December 86/January 87, Forecast section.

CHAPTER 10

1. Edmund A. Opitz, "The War on Poverty Revisited," *The Freeman*, February 1986, p. 48.

2. Charles Murray, *Losing Ground: American Social Policy 1950-1980*, (New York: Basic Books, 1984), pp. 56-66.

3. Ibid., pp. 164-65.

4. Ibid., pp. 24-40 and pp. 178-91.

5. Robert Woodson, "Poverty: Why Politics Can't Cure It," (Michigan: Hillsdale College, July 1988), *Imprimis*, Vol. 17, #7.

6. L. Gordon Crovitz, "A Primer on the ACLU," *The Wall Street Journal*, October 3, 1988, p. A20.

7. Janice C. Simpson, "A Settlement House Has New Constituency But Same Old Mission, *The Wall Street Journal*, January 23, 1987, p. 1.

8. Ibid.

9. Ilana DeBare, "County May End Cash Aid For Homeless," *The Sacramento Bee*, September 5, 1988, p. B1.

10. Ibid., p. B2.

11. Victor Giminian, "Assisting the Homeless: Grants or a 'Poorhouse'?" *The Sacramento Bee*, December 13, 1988, p. B5.

12. Lawrence C. Irby, "County Pulls Welcome Mat From Under Poor," *The Sacramento Union*, December 18, 1988, p. 24.

13. DeBare, op. cit., p. B2.

CHAPTER 11

1. Robert G. Wearner, John Leland, "Man Behind the Giants," *Liberty*, March/April 1987, p. 22.

2. Frank Van Der Linden, "Reagan Pounds The Desk," *The Sacramento Union*, October 25, 1987, editorial page.

3. W. Clark Durant, III, "Legal Services or Political Harassment?" *Human Events*, September 5, 1987, pp. 11-12.

4. James T. Bennett and Thomas J. DiLorenzo, "Destroying Democracy: How Government Funds Partisan Politics" (Washington, DC: Cato Institute, 1985).

5. Ibid., p. 306.

6. Ibid., pp. 306-07.

7. Walter Williams, "You Pay for this Nonsense," *The Sacramento Union*, October 20, 1986, p. A8.

8. Kathleen B. deBettencourt, "Legal Services Corporation and the Impact on the Family: A Preliminary Report" (Washington, DC: Legal Services Corporation, Office of Policy Development, March 1988).

9. Ibid., pp. 29-30.

10. Bennett and DiLorenzo, op. cit., p. 328.

11. Thomas J. Opsut, Interim President, Legal Services Corporation, "Study of LSC Involvement in Redistricting," submitted to Senator Orrin Hatch, cover letter dated February 27, 1985, p. 3.

12. Thomas DiLorenzo, "The Anti-Business Campaign of the Legal Services Corporation" (St. Louis, MO: Center for the Study of American Business, Washington University, April 1988), #85, p. 3.

13. Ibid.

14. Ibid., p. 12.

15. David Hoppe, "Without Reforms, The Legal Services Corporation Bill Deserves a Veto" (Washington, DC: The Heritage Foundation, September 23, 1988), *Executive Memorandum #214*.

16. Bennett and DiLorenzo, "Poverty, Politics and Jurisprudence: Illegalities at the Legal Services Corporation," *The Robber Barons of the Poor?* (Washington, DC: Washington Legal Foundation, 1985), p. 128.

17. Hoppe, op. cit., p. 2.

18. Bennett, op. cit., p. 309.

CHAPTER 12

1. Thomas Jefferson, letter to Thomas Cooper, November 29, 1802, *The Jeffersonian Cyclopedia*, p. 271.

2. Public opinion survey, "Public Attitudes Toward Taxation in California" (Los Angeles, California: Haug Associates, Inc., February 1973), a copy of which is maintained in The Tax/Expenditure Library, Lowe Institute of Political Economy, Claremont McKenna College, Claremont, CA.

3. Thomas G. Donlan, "Shooting the Works: A Surprising View From a Panel on Our Infrastructure," *Barron's,* (February 1, 1988), p. 67.

CHAPTER 13

1. Thomas Jefferson, "Autobiography," *The Writings of Thomas Jefferson*, ed. Paul L. Ford, vol. 1, p. 118 (1892).

2. "Budget of the United States Government, 1989," pp. 6g-30, 6g-38.

3. Bruce Bartlett, "The Chicken Little Theory of the Vanishing Middle Class," (Washington, DC: The Heritage Foundation, The Thomas A. Roe Institute for Economic Policy Studies, April 13, 1987), *Backgrounder #574*.

4. Gen. Daniel O. Graham (Ret.), "Deploy SDI and Balance the Budget" (Washington, DC: High Frontier, February 1987), position statement.

5. Robert W. Poole, Jr., "User-Friendly Air Traffic Control, Now," *The Wall Street Journal,* July 1, 1987, editorial page.

6. See for example: Stephen Moore, "The Highway Authorization Bill: Inviting a Presidential Veto" (Washington, DC: The Heritage Foundation, February 27, 1987), *Issue Bulletin #127*.

7. Edward H. Crane, "Beyond the Status Quo" (Washington, DC: Cato Institute, March 1, 1986), *Vital Speeches of the Day,* vol. LII, no. 10, p. 299.

CHAPTER 14

1. Thomas Jefferson, letter to John Taylor, November 26, 1798, Paul Leicester Ford, ed., *The Writings of Thomas Jefferson* (New York: G.P. Putnam's Sons, 1904), p. 481.
2. Report of the Committee on the Judiciary of the United States Senate on Senate Joint Resolution 58, "Balanced Budget-Tax Limitation Amendment," 97th Congress, First Session, July 10, 1981, Report #97-151, p. 3.

CHAPTER 16

1. Russell L. Caplan, *Constitutional Brinksmanship: Amending the Constitution by National Convention* (New York: Oxford University Press, 1988), pp. 27-28.
2. Ibid.
3. Ibid., p. 29.
4. Ibid., pp. 81-82.
5. Remarks of George Roberts to the author, May 1988, in Concord, NH.
6. Caplan, op. cit., pp. 95, 98-99.
7. Ibid., p. 42.
8. American Bar Association, "Amendment of the Constitution by the Convention Method under Article V," prepared by the Special Constitutional Convention Study Committee, 1974, p. 16.
9. United States Department of Justice, "Limited Constitutional Conventions under Article V of the United States Constitution" (Washington, DC: The Office of Legal Policy, September 10, 1987).
10. Caplan, op. cit., pp. 160-61.
11. American Bar Association, op. cit., p. 11.
12. U.S. Senator Sam Ervin, Chairman, Subcommittee on the Constitution, The Convention Method of Amending the Constitution, 66 Michigan Law Review 875, 883 (1968).
13. Griffin Bell, "Life, Liberty and the Call for a Balanced Budget," *The Detroit News*, November 5, 1985, p. 17A.

14. John Noonan (former Professor of Law, University of California School of Law, now Justice of the Ninth Circuit), testimony before the California State Assembly, February 15, 1979.

15. Prof. William Van Alstyne, Duke University Law School, The Limited Constitutional Convention, 1979 Duke Law Journal, 985-98.

16. Aaron Wildavsky, Political Science Department, Graduate School of Public Policy and Survey Research Center, University of California, Berkeley, "The Runaway Convention or Proving a Preposterous Negative," a paper prepared for the Taxpayers' Foundation (1983), p. 7.

17. Prof. Henry Campbell Black, Handbook of American Constitutional Law 45 (1927).

18. Paper delivered at the annual meeting of the Southern Political Science Association, Savannah, GA, November 12-13, 1982.

19. John T. Noonan, "Calling for a Constitutional Convention," *The Constitution,* September 1985, p, 16.

20. Phyllis Schlafly, *DAR,* January 1985; Gary Benoit, *The New American,* February 10, 1986.

21. "The Committee on the Constitutional System," ed. Donald L. Robinson, (1985: Westview Press, Colorado and London), p. 267 (the article was originally printed in *The Center,* 1980).

22. Phyllis Schlafly, *The Phyllis Schlafly Report,* September 1987.

23. Noonan, op. cit.

24. Caplan, op. cit., pp. 155, 148-49.

25. Ibid., pp. 161-62.

26. Ibid., p. x.

INDEX